SUPER EASY SONGBOOK

FOLKSONGS

ISBN 978-1-70515-242-3

HAL•LEONARD®

Copyright © 2021 by HAL LEONARD LLC
International Copyright Secured   All Rights Reserved

Visit Hal Leonard Online at
www.halleonard.com

Contact us:
Hal Leonard
7777 West Bluemound Road
Milwaukee, WI 53213
Email: info@halleonard.com

In Europe, contact:
Hal Leonard Europe Limited
42 Wigmore Street
Marylebone, London, W1U 2RN
Email: info@halleonardeurope.com

In Australia, contact:
Hal Leonard Australia Pty. Ltd.
4 Lentara Court
Cheltenham, Victoria, 3192 Australia
Email: info@halleonard.com.au

Aloha Oe

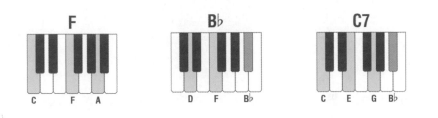

Words and Music by
Queen Liliuokalani

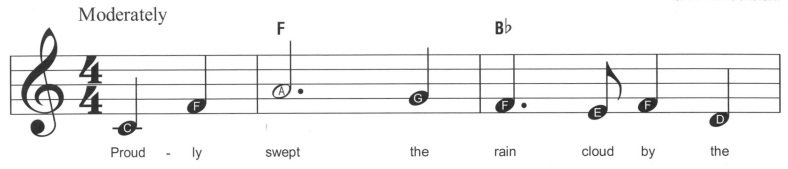

Proud - ly swept the rain cloud by the

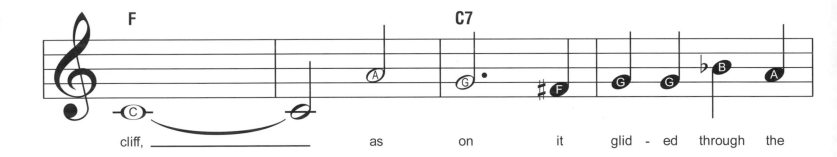

cliff, _____ as on it glid - ed through the

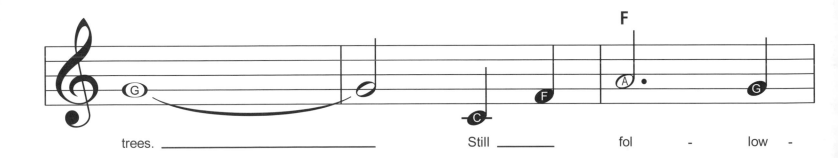

trees. _____ Still _____ fol - low -

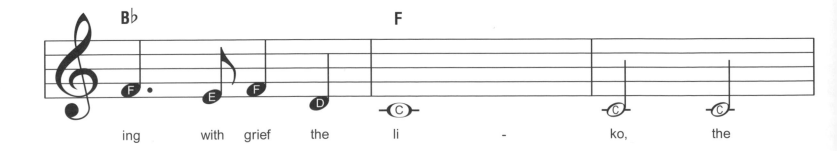

ing with grief the li - ko, the

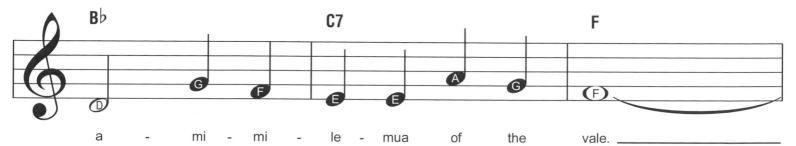

a - mi - mi - le - mua of the vale. _____

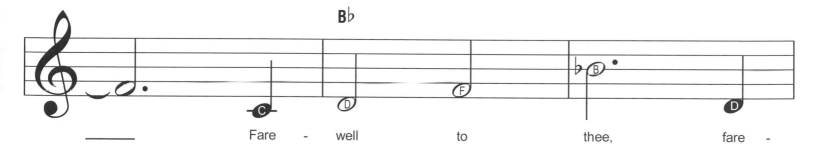

_____ Fare - well to thee, fare -

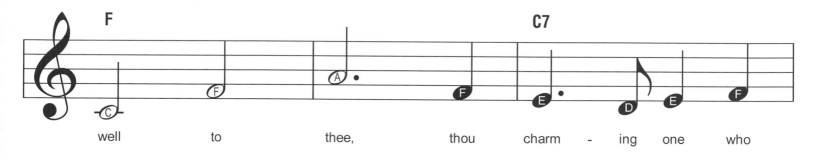

well to thee, thou charm - ing one who

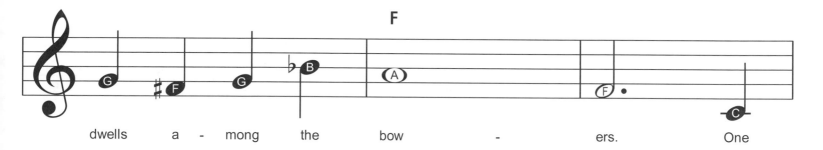

dwells a - mong the bow - ers. One

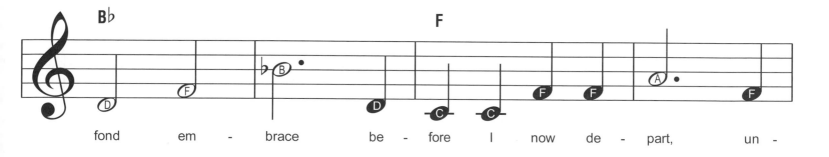

fond em - brace be - fore I now de - part, un -

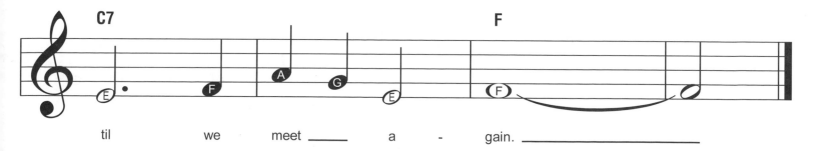

til we meet _____ a - gain. _____

Animal Fair

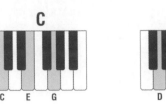

American Folksong

Auld Lang Syne

Words by Robert Burns
Traditional Scottish Melody

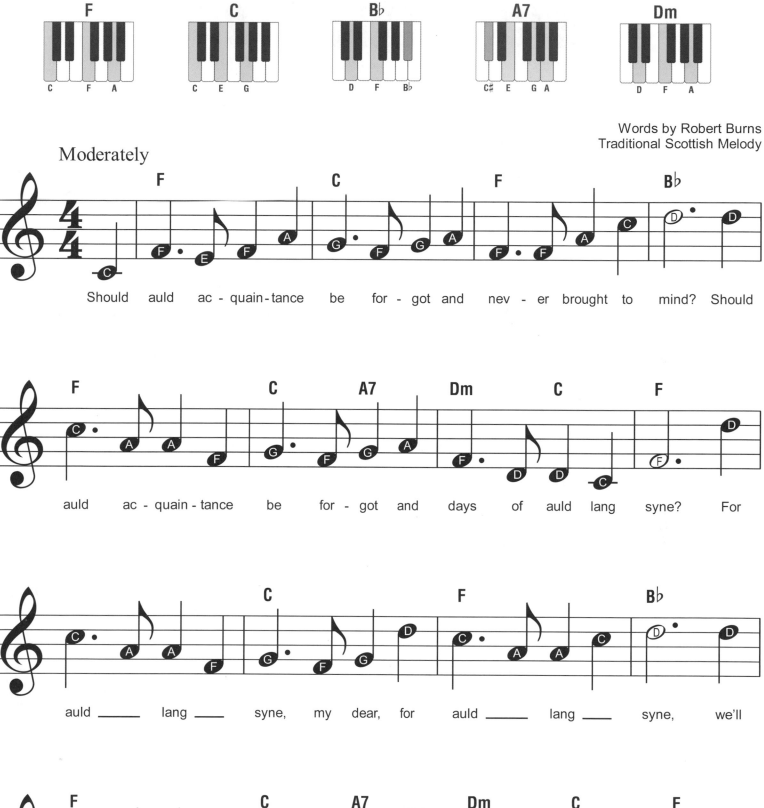

Should auld ac-quain-tance be for-got and nev-er brought to mind? Should

auld ac-quain-tance be for-got and days of auld lang syne? For

auld ____ lang ____ syne, my dear, for auld ____ lang ____ syne, we'll

take a cup of kind-ness yet, for ____ auld ____ lang ____ syne.

The Ash Grove

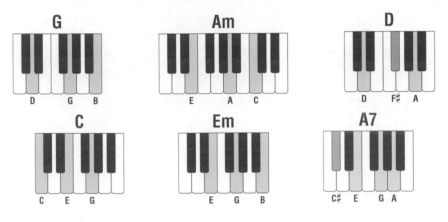

Old Welsh Air

Warmly

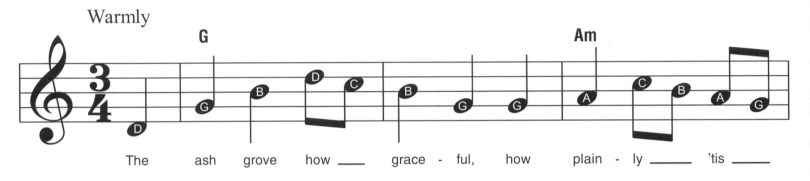

The ash grove how ___ grace - ful, how plain - ly ___ 'tis ___

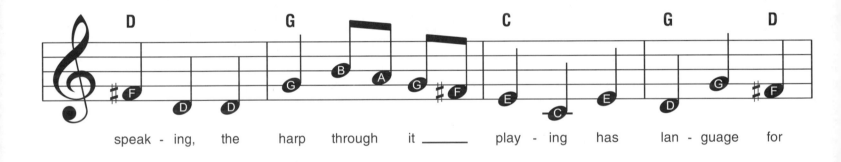

speak - ing, the harp through it ___ play - ing has lan - guage for

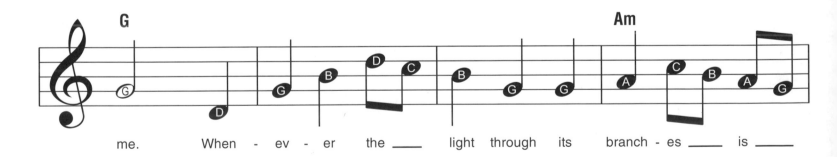

me. When - ev - er the ___ light through its branch - es ___ is ___

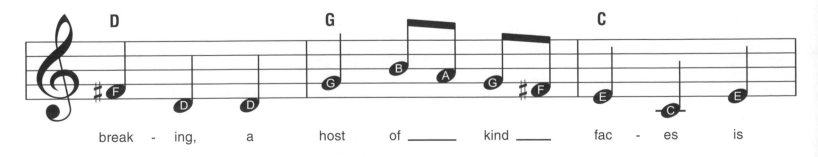

break - ing, a host of ___ kind ___ fac - es is

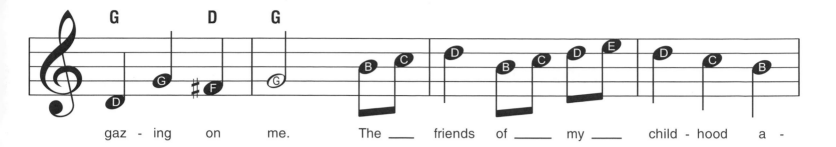

gaz - ing on me. The ___ friends of ___ my ___ child - hood a -

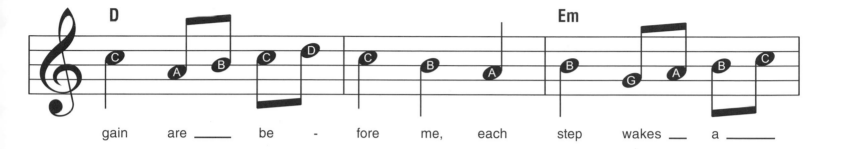

gain are ___ be - fore me, each step wakes ___ a ___

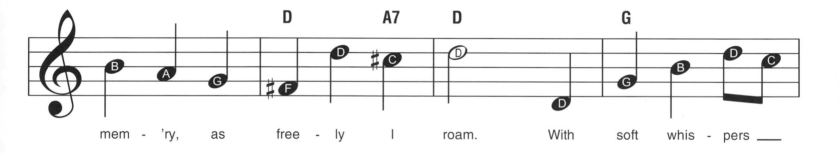

mem - 'ry, as free - ly I roam. With soft whis - pers ___

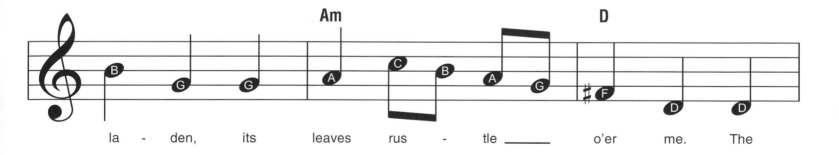

la - den, its leaves rus - tle ___ o'er me. The

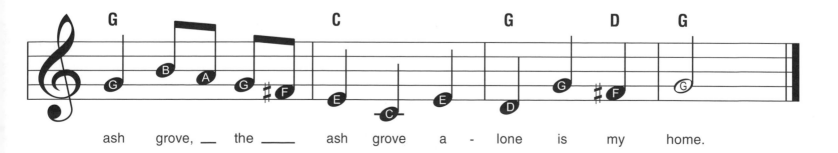

ash grove, ___ the ___ ash grove a - lone is my home.

Aura Lee

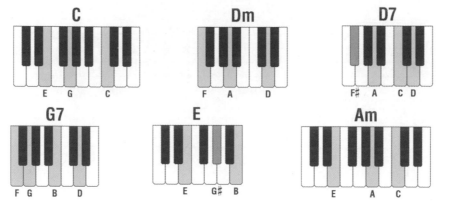

Words by W.W. Fosdick
Music by George R. Poulton

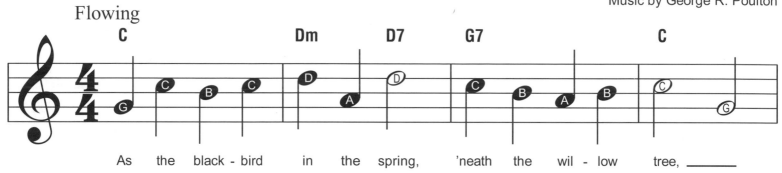

As the black - bird in the spring, 'neath the wil - low tree, _____

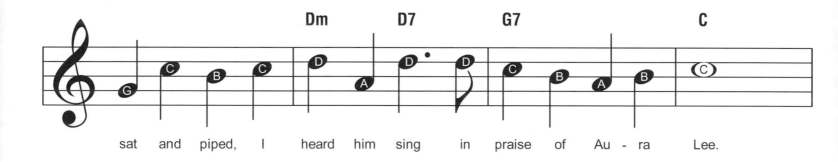

sat and piped, I heard him sing in praise of Au - ra Lee.

Au - ra Lee, Au - ra Lee, maid with gold - en hair,

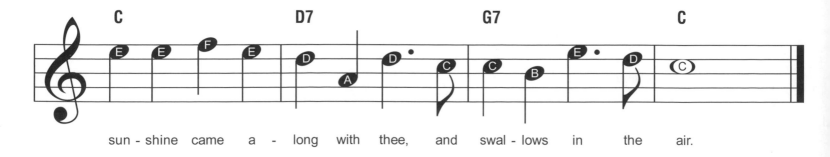

sun - shine came a - long with thee, and swal - lows in the air.

Blow the Man Down

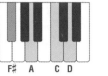

Traditional Sea Chantey

The Band Played On

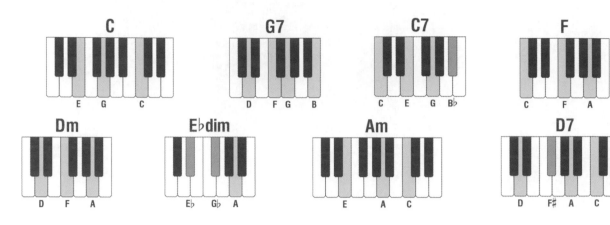

Words by John E. Palmer
Music by Charles B. Ward

Flowing

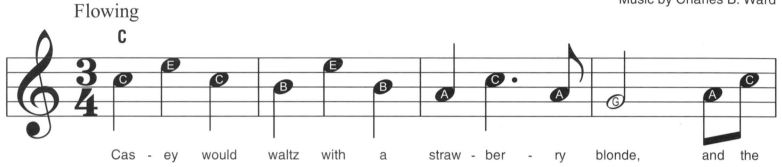

Cas - ey would waltz with a straw - ber - ry blonde, and the

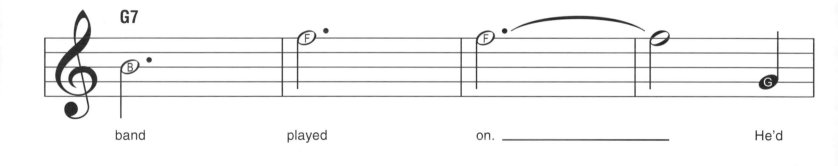

band played on. _____ He'd

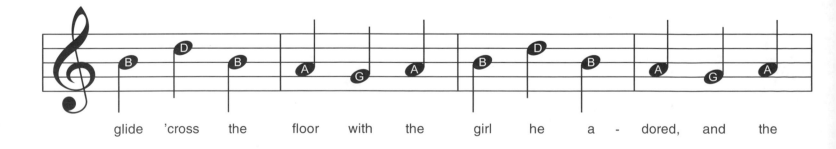

glide 'cross the floor with the girl he a - dored, and the

13

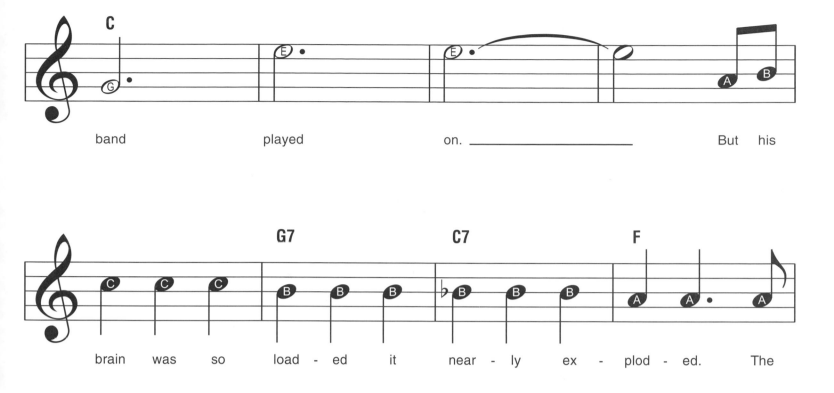

band played on. _____ But his

brain was so load - ed it near - ly ex - plod - ed. The

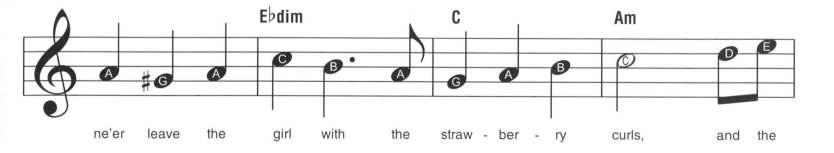

poor girl would shake with a - larm. _____ He'd

ne'er leave the girl with the straw - ber - ry curls, and the

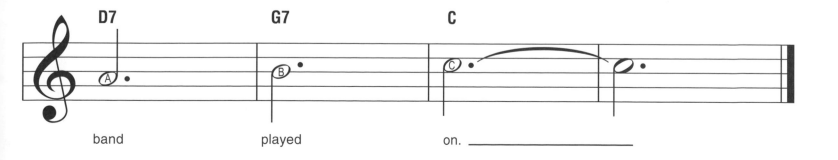

band played on. _____

Beautiful Brown Eyes

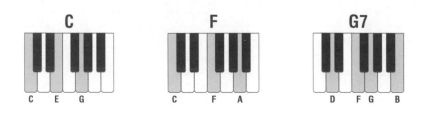

Traditional

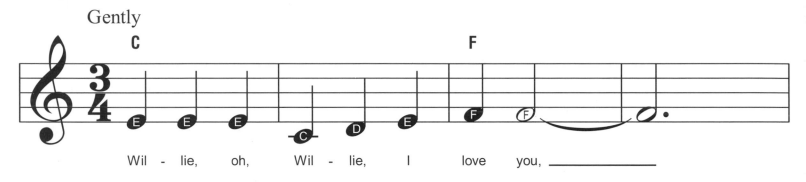

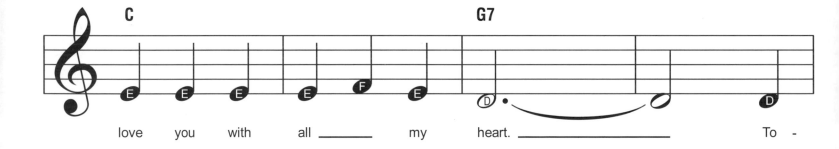

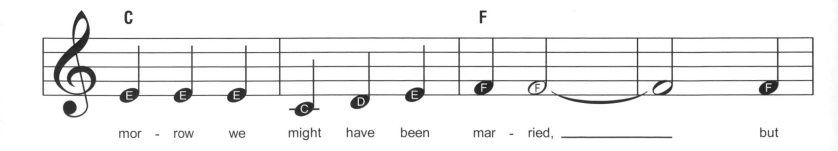

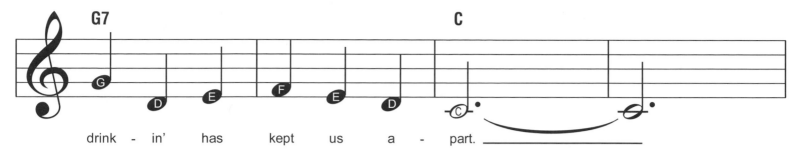

drink - in' has kept us a - part. _____

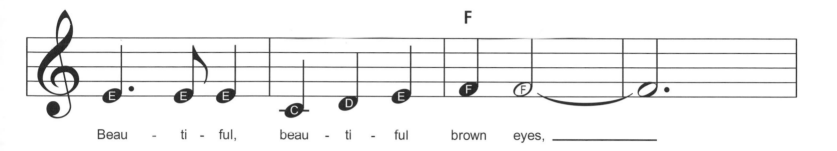

Beau - ti - ful, beau - ti - ful brown eyes, _____

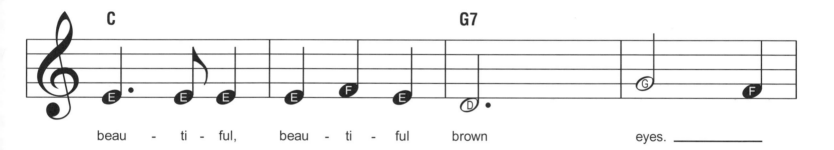

beau - ti - ful, beau - ti - ful brown eyes. _____

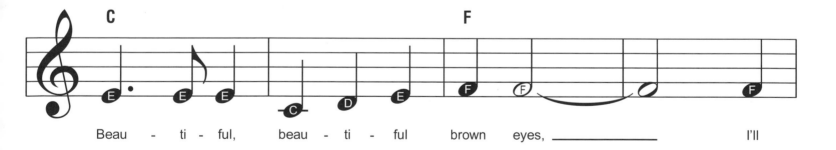

Beau - ti - ful, beau - ti - ful brown eyes, _____ I'll

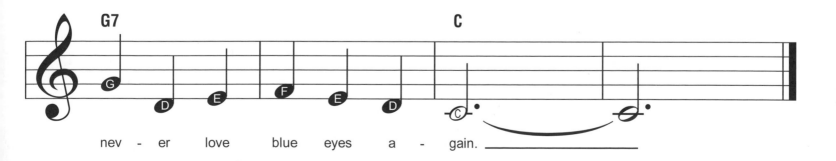

nev - er love blue eyes a - gain. _____

Beautiful Dreamer

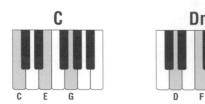
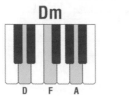
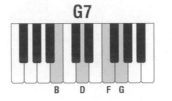
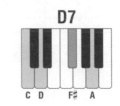
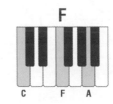

Words and Music by
Stephen C. Foster

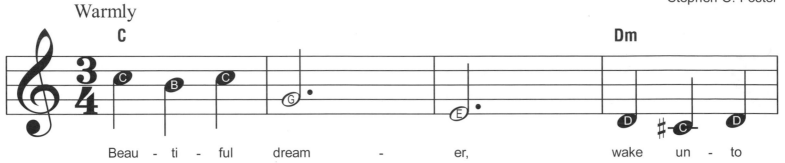

Beau - ti - ful dream - er, wake un - to

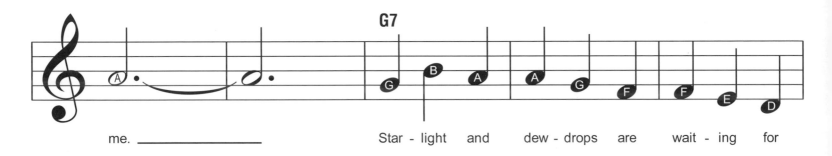

me. _____ Star - light and dew - drops are wait - ing for

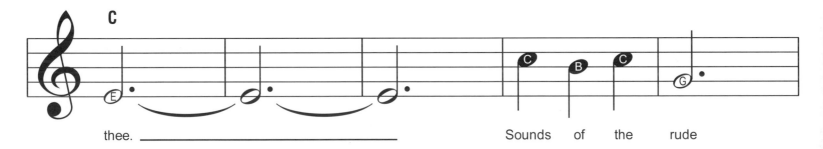

thee. _____ Sounds of the rude

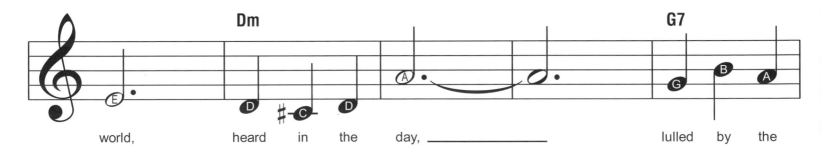

world, heard in the day, _____ lulled by the

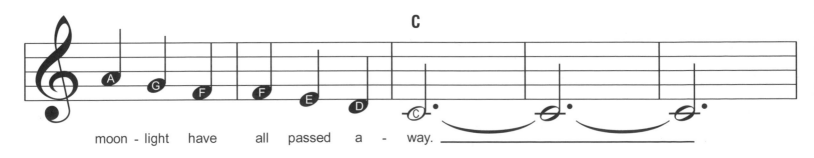

moon - light have all passed a - way. _____

17

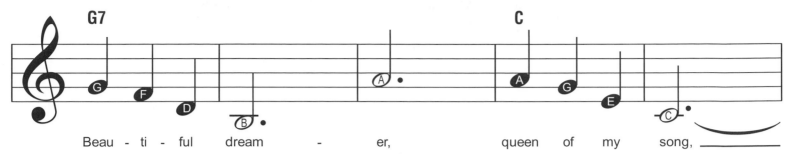

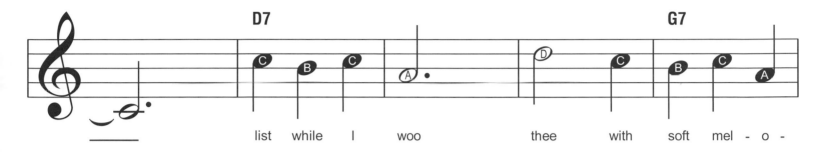

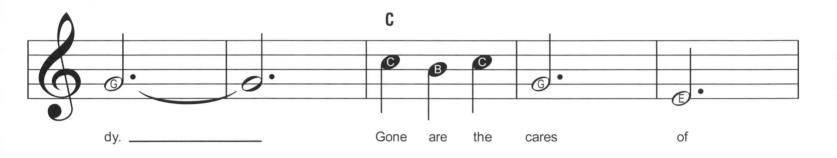

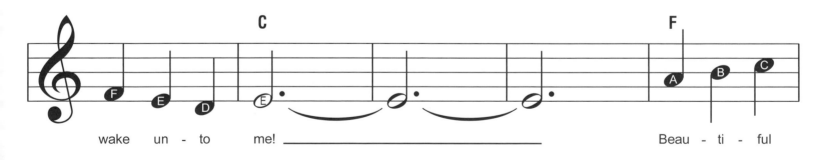

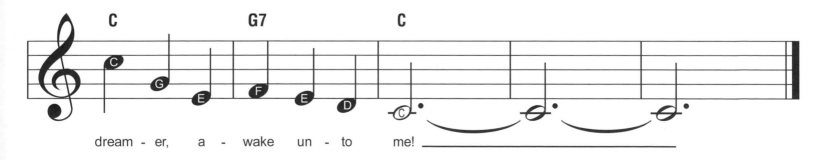

Believe Me, If All Those Endearing Young Charms

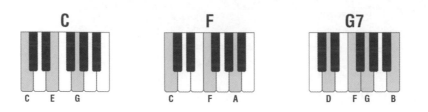

Words and Music by
Thomas Moore

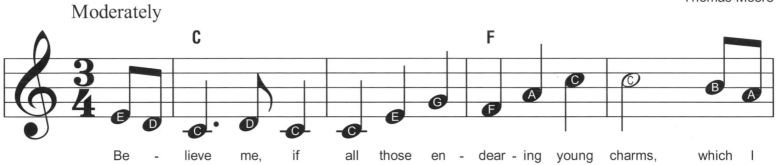

Be - lieve me, if all those en - dear - ing young charms, which I

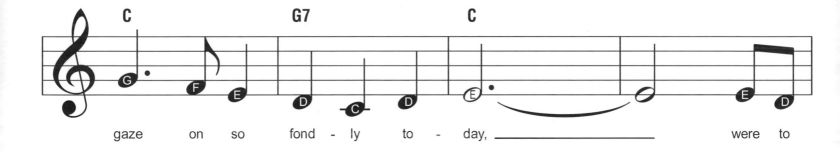

gaze on so fond - ly to - day, _____ were to

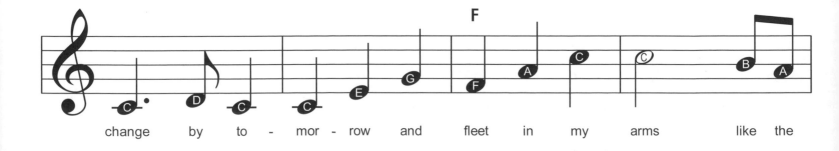

change by to - mor - row and fleet in my arms like the

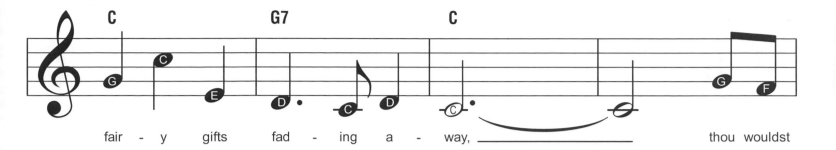

fair - y gifts fad - ing a - way, _____ thou wouldst

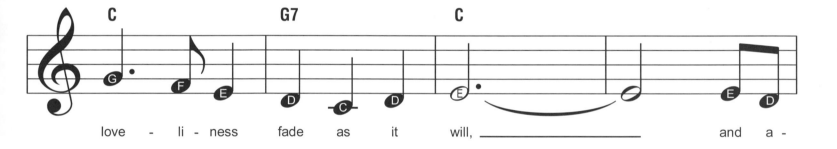

still be a - dored as this mo - ment thou art. Let thy

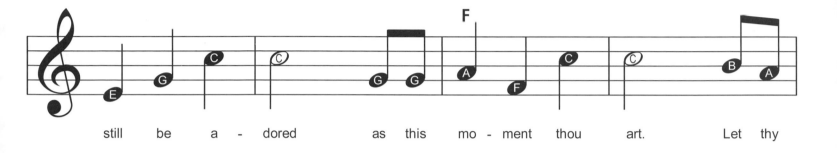

love - li - ness fade as it will, _____ and a -

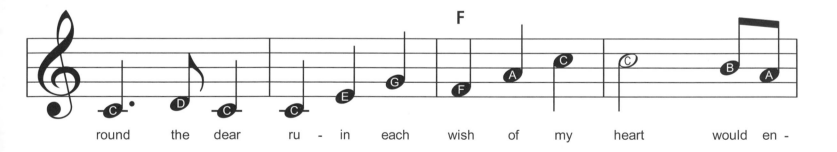

round the dear ru - in each wish of my heart would en -

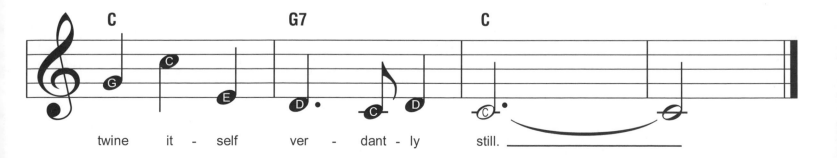

twine it - self ver - dant - ly still. _____

The Blue Bells of Scotland

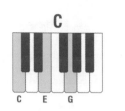
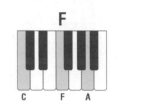
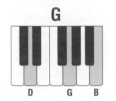
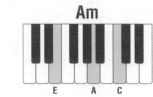
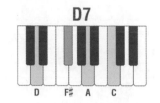

Words and Music attributed to
Mrs. Jordon

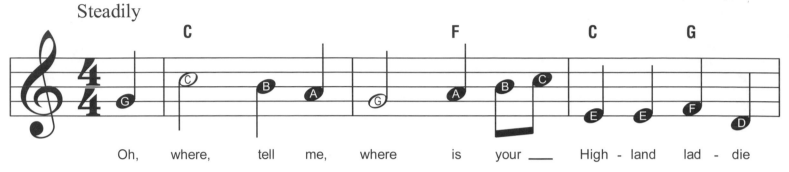

Oh, where, tell me, where is your ___ High - land lad - die

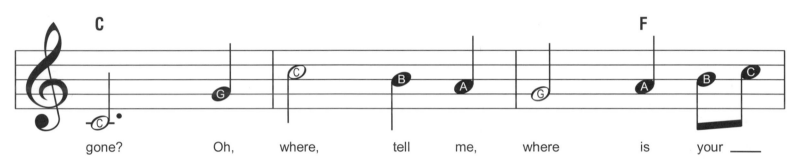

gone? Oh, where, tell me, where is your ___

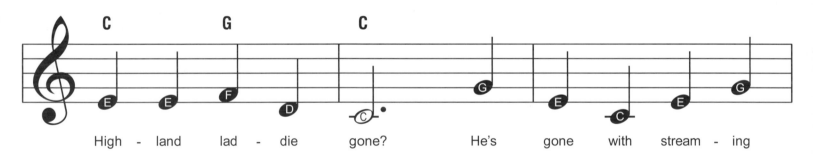

High - land lad - die gone? He's gone with stream - ing

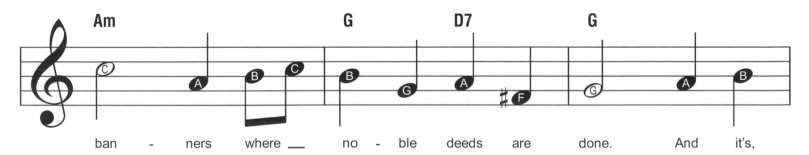

ban - ners where ___ no - ble deeds are done. And it's,

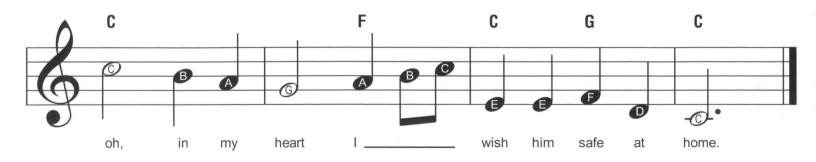

oh, in my heart I _____ wish him safe at home.

Cindy

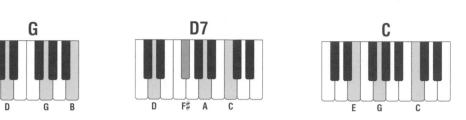

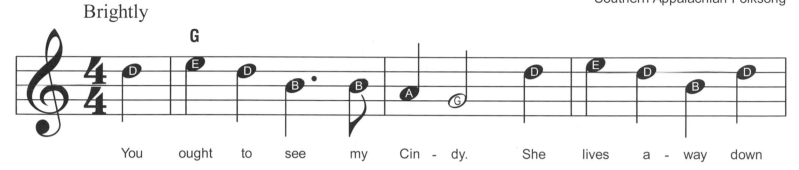

Southern Appalachian Folksong

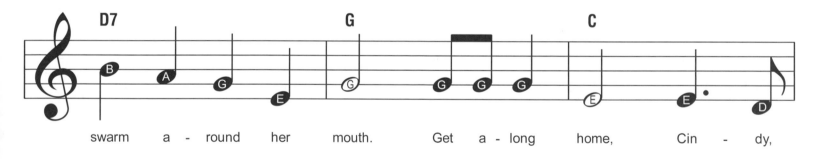

You ought to see my Cin - dy. She lives a - way down

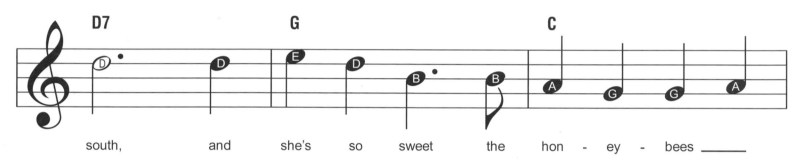

south, and she's so sweet the hon - ey - bees _____

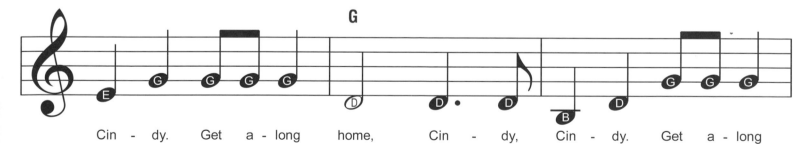

swarm a - round her mouth. Get a - long home, Cin - dy,

Cin - dy. Get a - long home, Cin - dy, Cin - dy. Get a - long

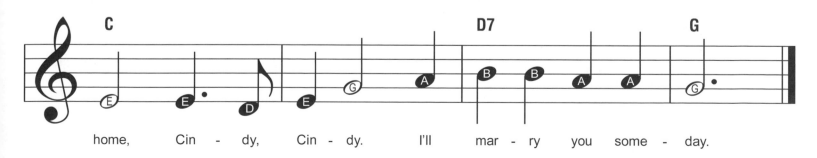

home, Cin - dy, Cin - dy. I'll mar - ry you some - day.

Buffalo Gals
(Won't You Come Out Tonight?)

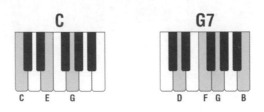

Words and Music by
Cool White (John Hodges)

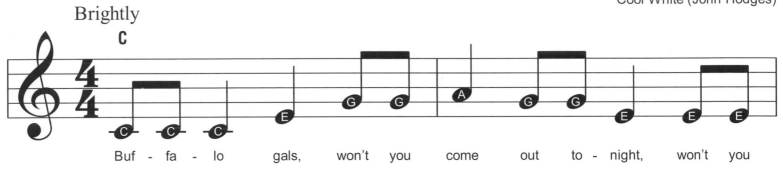

Buf - fa - lo gals, won't you come out to - night, won't you

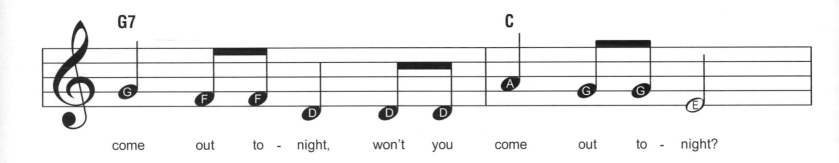

come out to - night, won't you come out to - night?

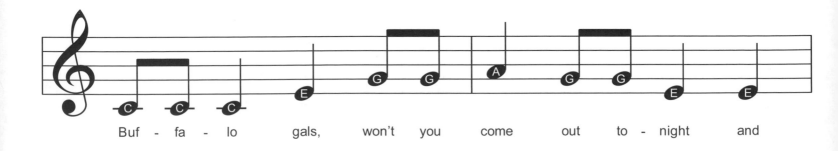

Buf - fa - lo gals, won't you come out to - night and

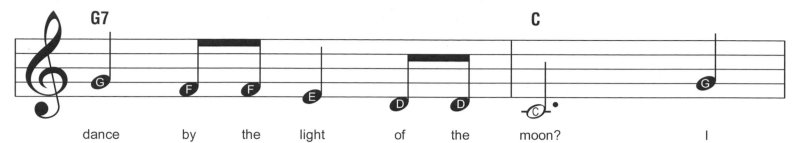

dance   by   the   light   of   the   moon?   I

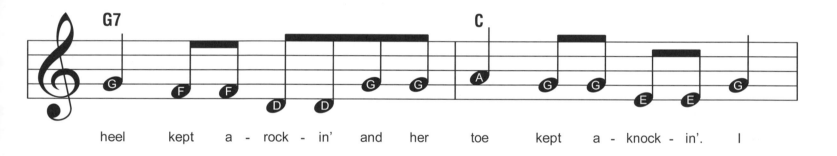

danced   with   a   gal   with   a   hole   in   her   stock - ing   and   her

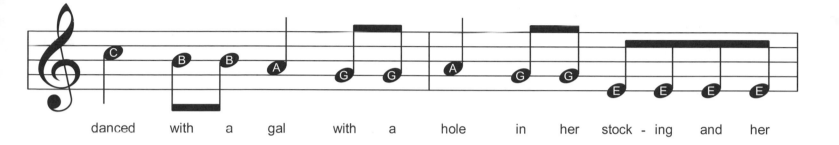

heel   kept   a - rock - in'   and   her   toe   kept   a - knock - in'.   I

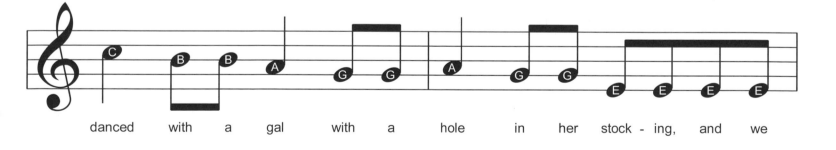

danced   with   a   gal   with   a   hole   in   her   stock - ing,   and   we

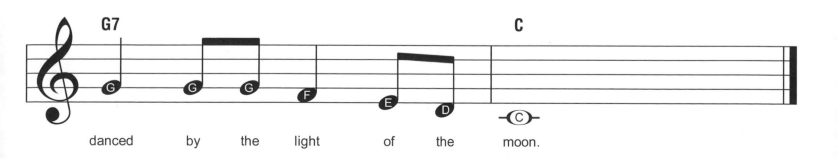

danced   by   the   light   of   the   moon.

Chiapanecas

Mexican Folk Song

Quickly

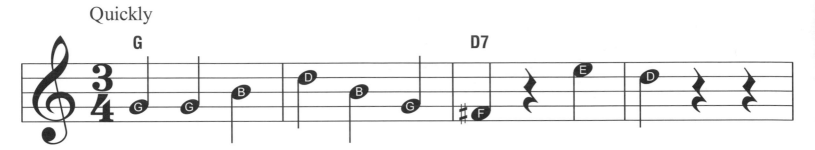

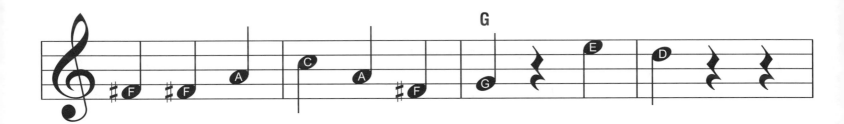

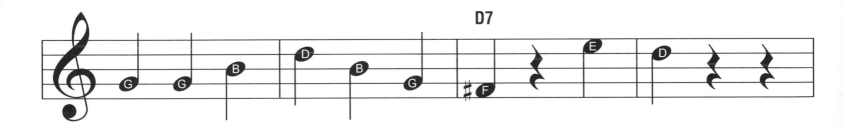

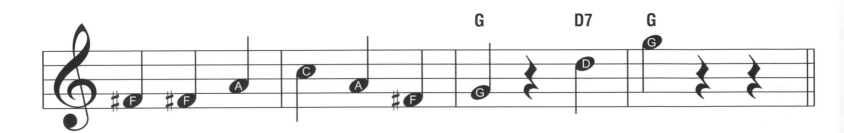

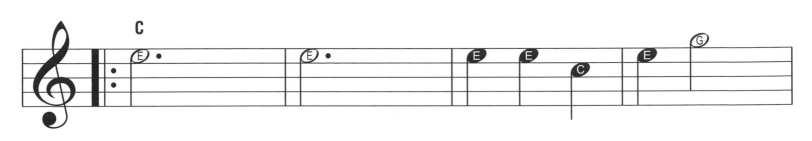

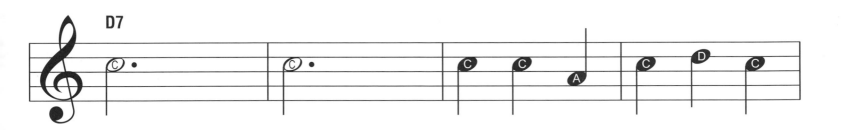

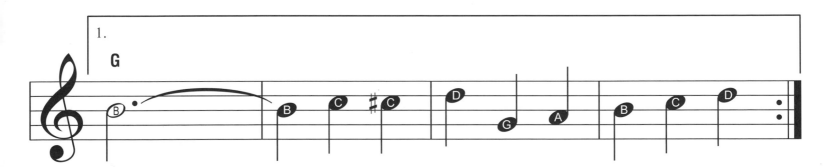

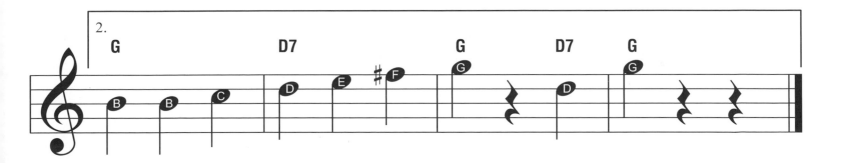

(Oh, My Darling)
Clementine

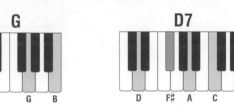

Words and Music by
Percy Montrose

Frankie and Johnny

Anonymous Blues Ballad

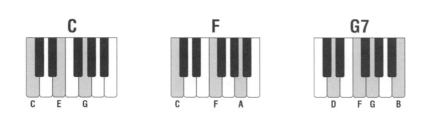

Cockles and Mussels
(Molly Malone)

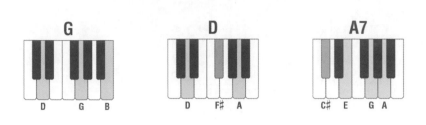

Traditional Irish Folksong

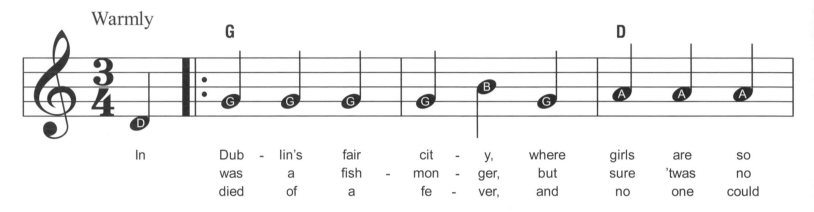

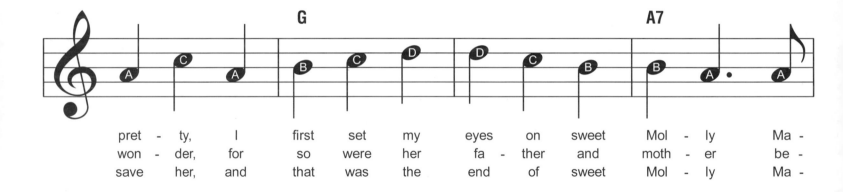

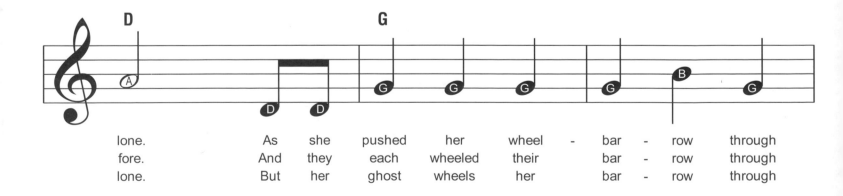

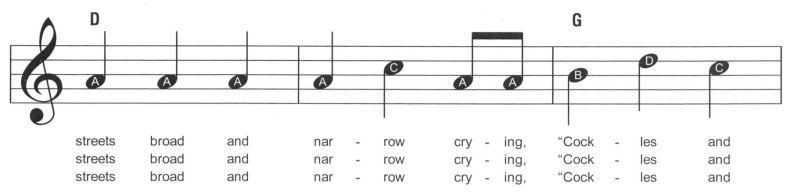

streets broad and nar - row cry - ing, "Cock - les and
streets broad and nar - row cry - ing, "Cock - les and
streets broad and nar - row cry - ing, "Cock - les and

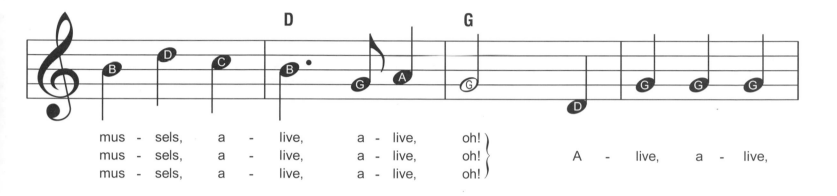

mus - sels, a - live, a - live, oh! } A - live, a - live,
mus - sels, a - live, a - live, oh!
mus - sels, a - live, a - live, oh!

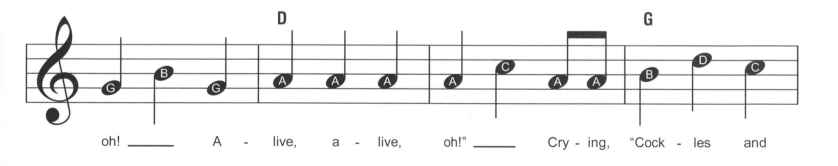

oh! _____ A - live, a - live, oh!" _____ Cry - ing, "Cock - les and

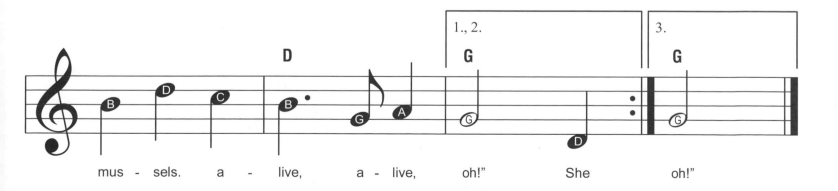

1., 2.

3.

mus - sels, a - live, a - live, oh!" She oh!"

Danny Boy

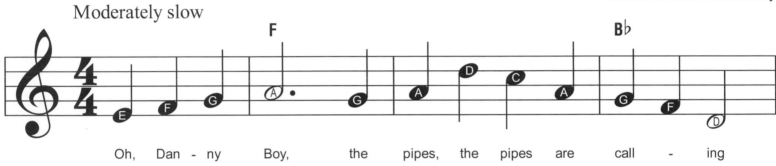

Words by Frederick Edward Weatherly
Traditional Irish Folk Melody

Moderately slow

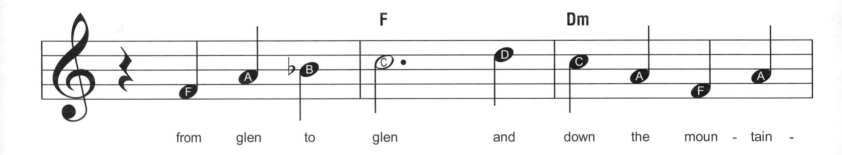

Oh, Dan - ny Boy, the pipes, the pipes are call - ing

from glen to glen and down the moun - tain -

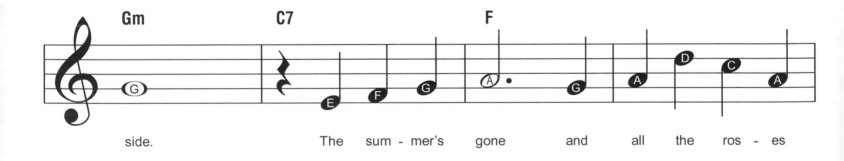

side. The sum - mer's gone and all the ros - es

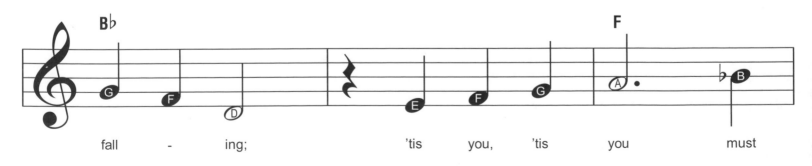

fall - ing; 'tis you, 'tis you must

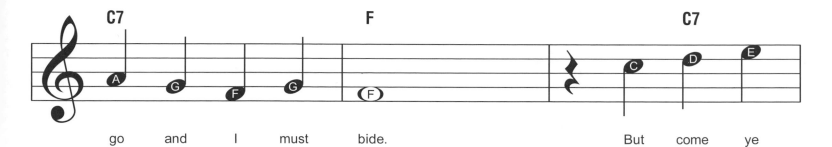

go and I must bide. But come ye

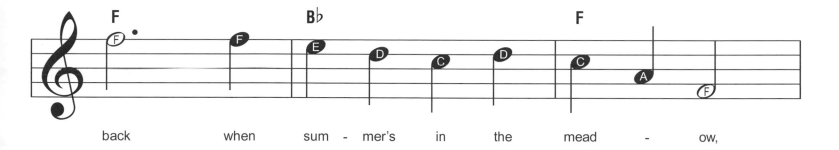

back when sum - mer's in the mead - ow,

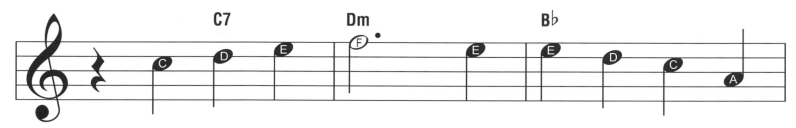

or when the val - ley's hushed and white with

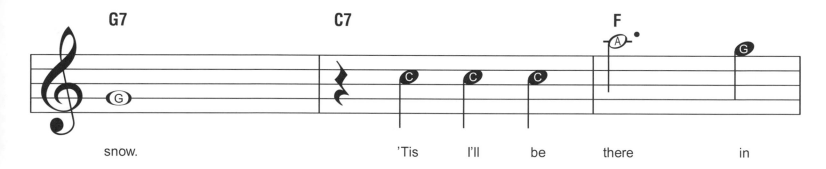

snow. 'Tis I'll be there in

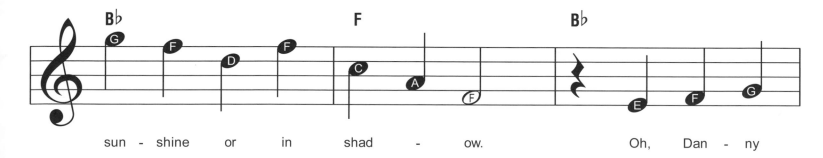

sun - shine or in shad - ow. Oh, Dan - ny

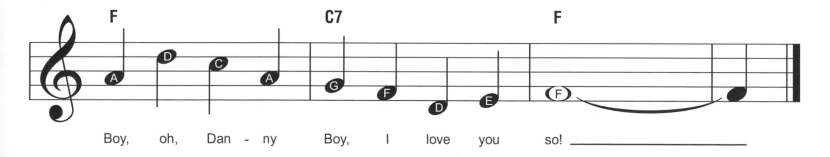

Boy, oh, Dan - ny Boy, I love you so! _____

Deep River

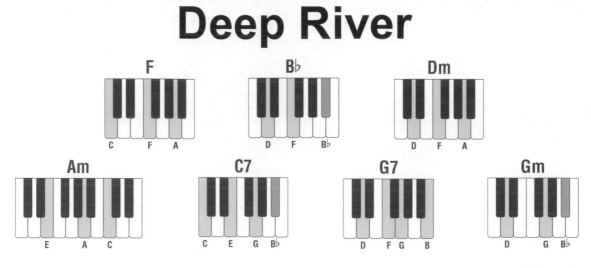

African-American Spiritual
Based on Joshua 3

Soulfully

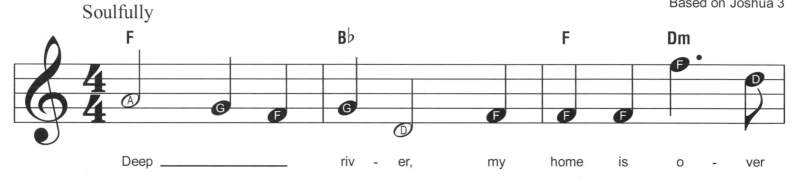

Deep _____ riv - er, my home is o - ver

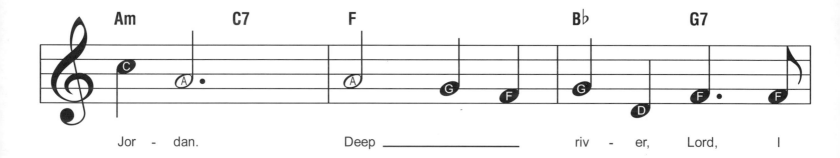

Jor - dan. Deep _____ riv - er, Lord, I

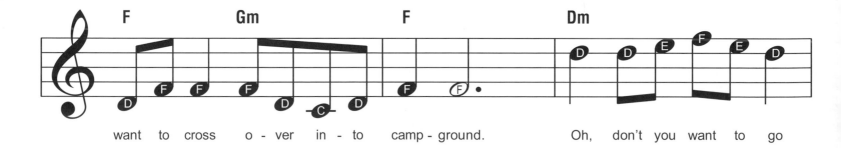

want to cross o - ver in - to camp - ground. Oh, don't you want to go

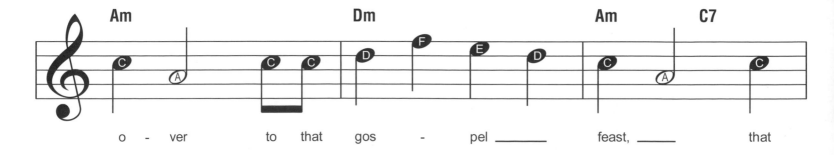

o - ver to that gos - pel _____ feast, _____ that

33

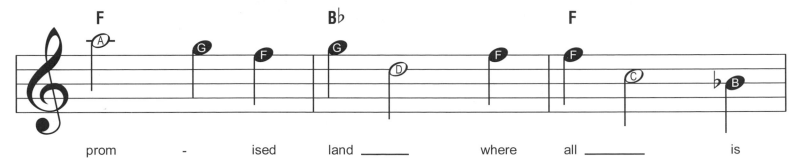

prom - ised land _____ where all _____ is

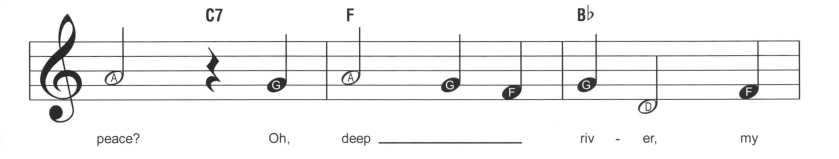

peace? Oh, deep _____ riv - er, my

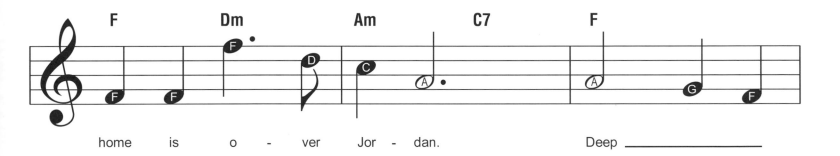

home is o - ver Jor - dan. Deep _____

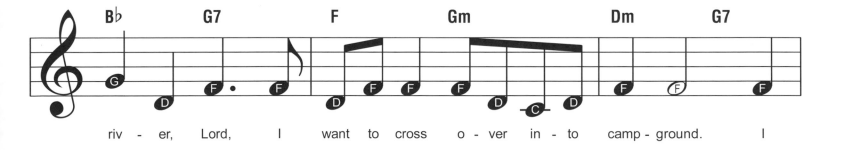

riv - er, Lord, I want to cross o - ver in - to camp - ground. I

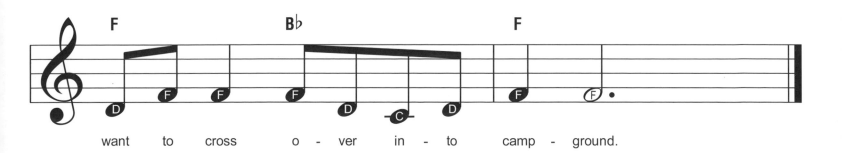

want to cross o - ver in - to camp - ground.

Down by the Riverside

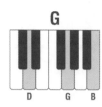
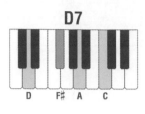

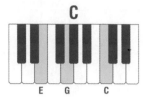

African-American Spiritual

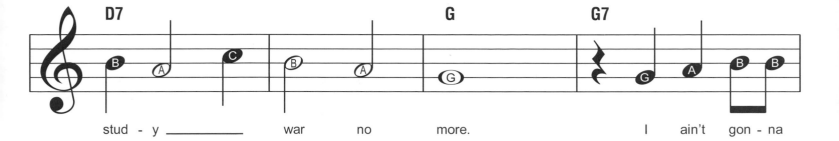

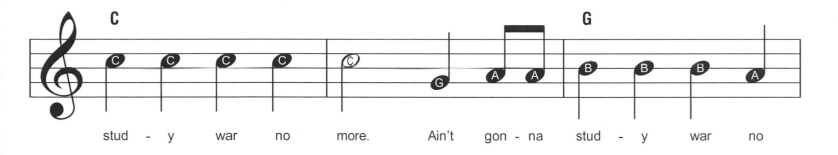

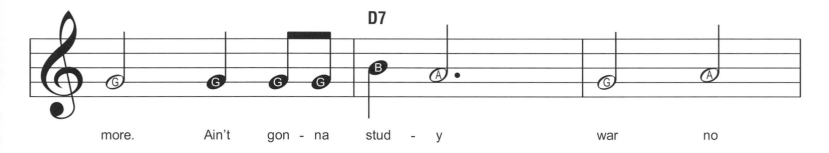

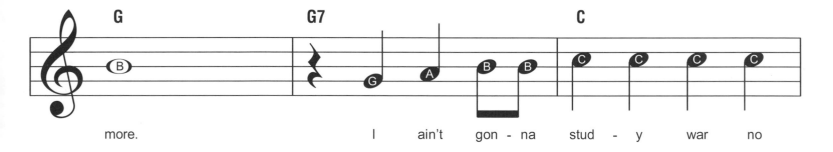

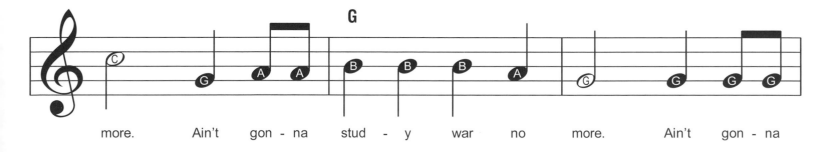

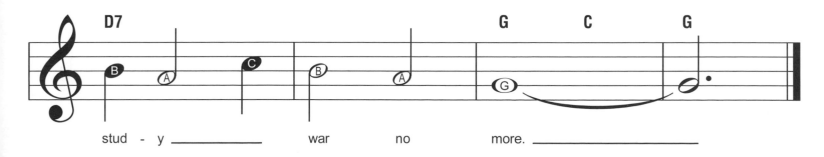

Down in the Valley

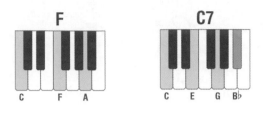

Traditional American Folksong

Moderately

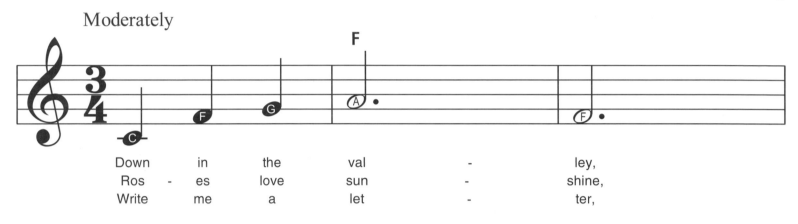

Down in the val - ley,
Ros - es love sun - shine,
Write me a let - ter,

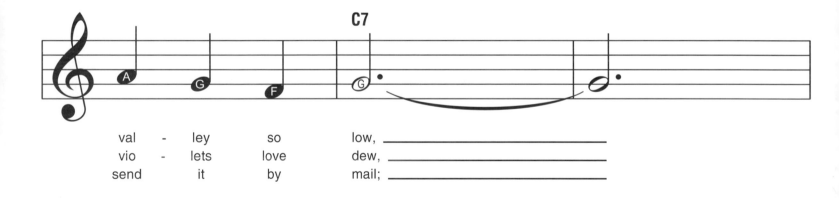

val - ley so low, _____
vio - lets love dew, _____
send it by mail; _____

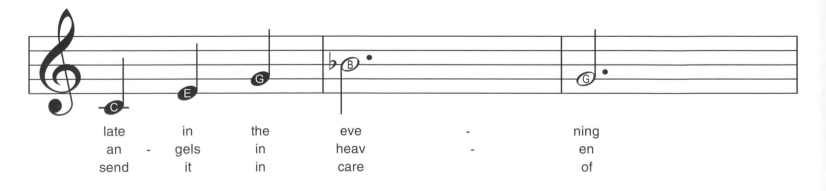

late in the eve - ning
an - gels in heav - en
send it in care of

Drink to Me Only with Thine Eyes

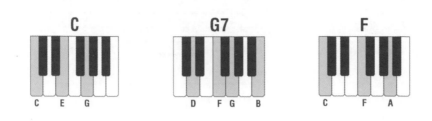

Lyrics by Ben Jonson
Traditional Music

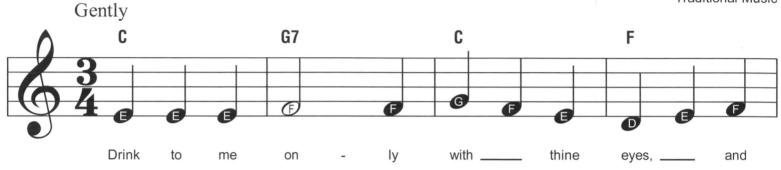

Drink to me on - ly with _____ thine eyes, _____ and

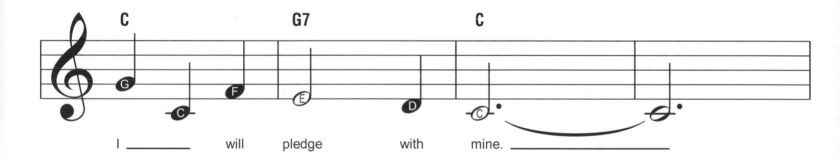

I _____ will pledge with mine. _____

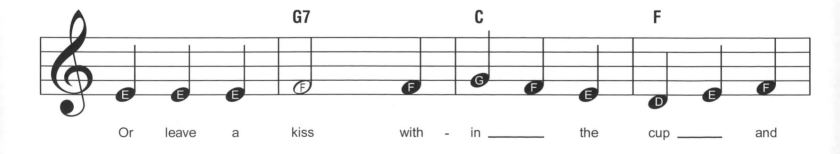

Or leave a kiss with - in _____ the cup _____ and

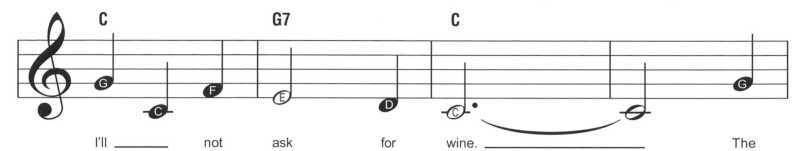

I'll _____ not ask for wine. _____ The

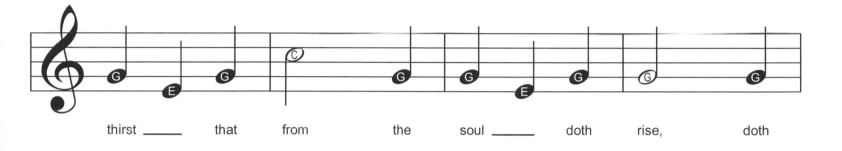

thirst _____ that from the soul _____ doth rise, doth

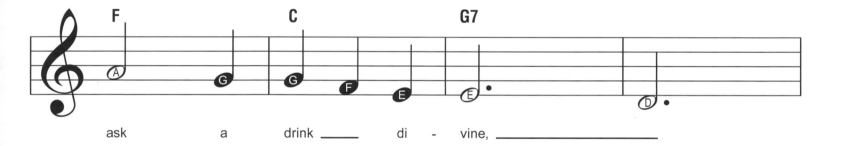

ask a drink _____ di - vine, _____

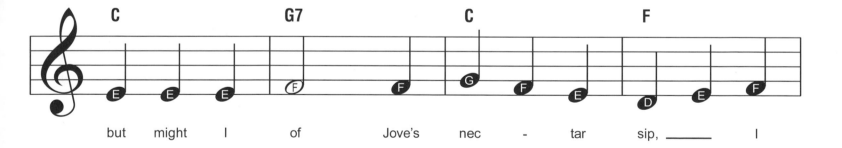

but might I of Jove's nec - tar sip, _____ I

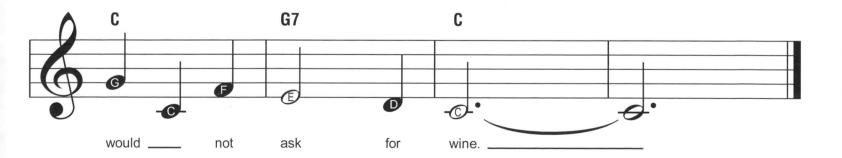

would _____ not ask for wine. _____

The Erie Canal

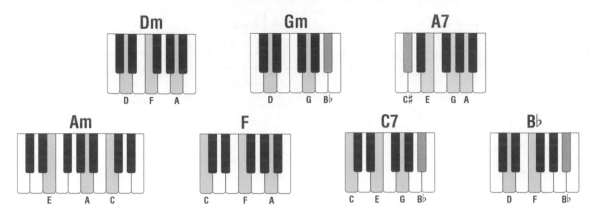

Traditional New York Work Song

Moderately

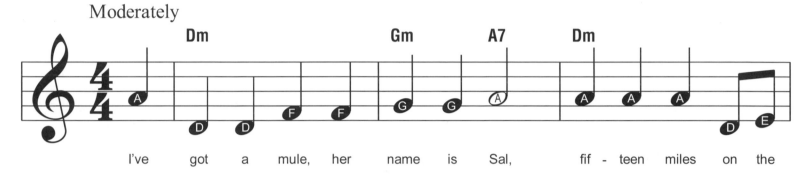

I've got a mule, her name is Sal, fif - teen miles on the

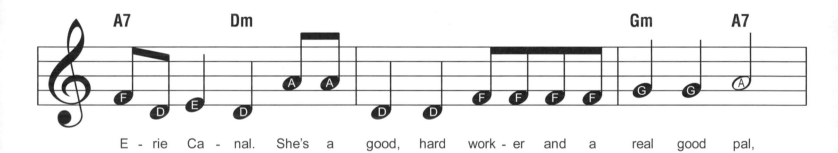

E - rie Ca - nal. She's a good, hard work - er and a real good pal,

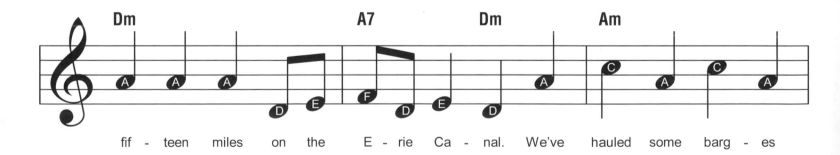

fif - teen miles on the E - rie Ca - nal. We've hauled some barg - es

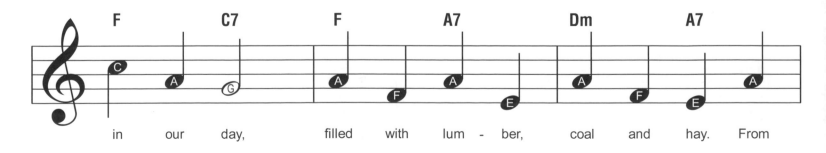

in our day, filled with lum - ber, coal and hay. From

41

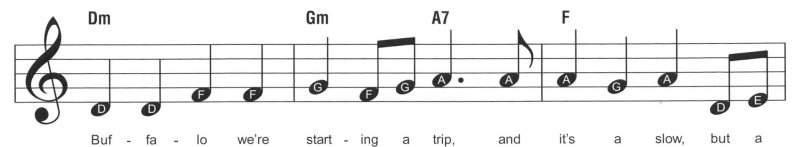

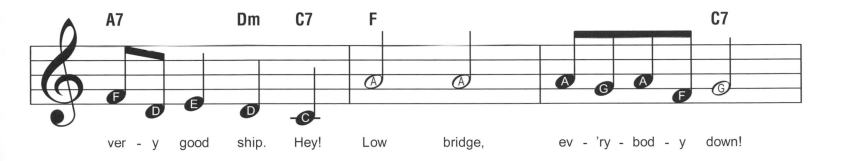

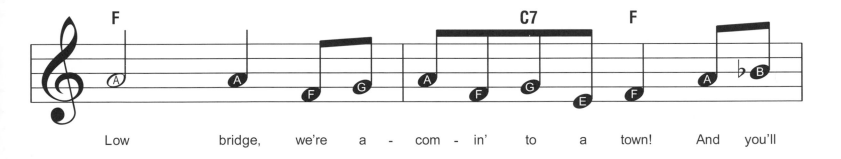

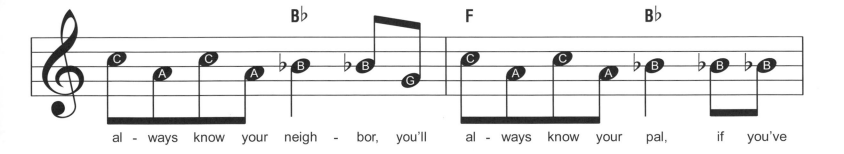

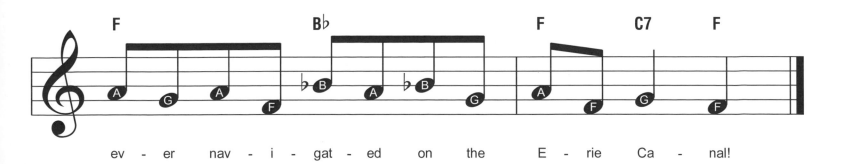

The Foggy, Foggy Dew

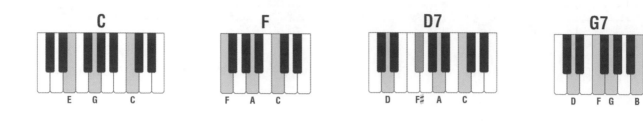

Traditional

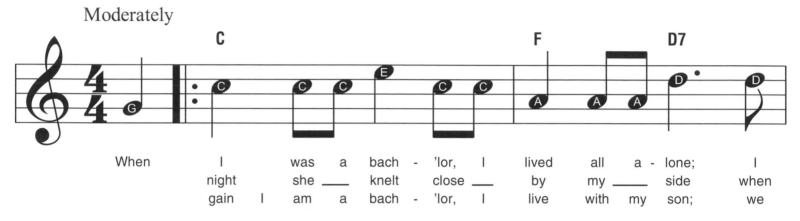

Moderately

When I was a bach - 'lor, I lived all a - lone; I
night she ___ knelt close ___ by my ___ side when
gain I am a bach - 'lor, I live with my son; when we

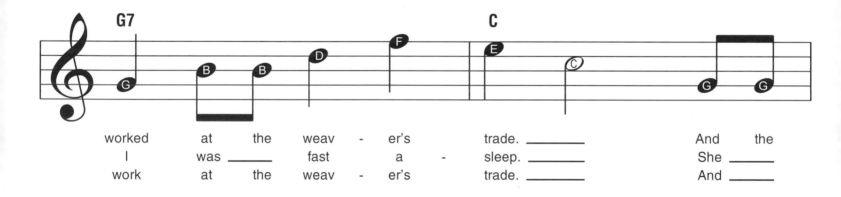

worked at the weav - er's trade. _____ And the
I was ___ fast a - sleep. _____ She ___
work at the weav - er's trade. _____ And _____

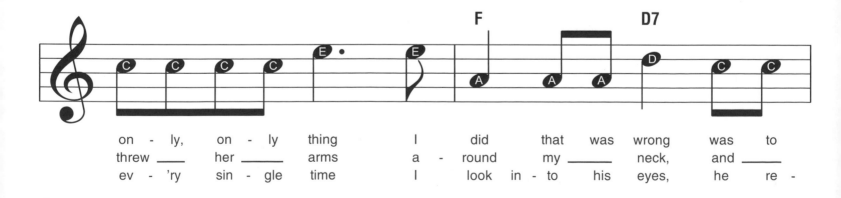

on - ly, on - ly thing I did that was wrong, was to
threw ___ her ___ arms a - round my ___ neck, and _____
ev - 'ry sin - gle time I look in - to his eyes, he re -

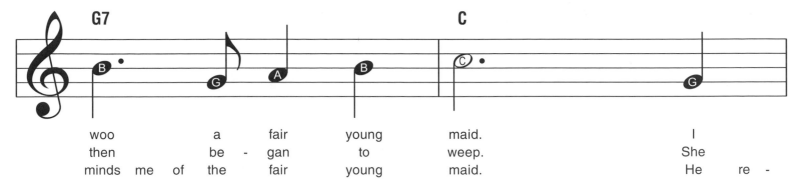

woo a fair young maid. I
then be - gan to weep. She
minds me of the fair young maid. He re -

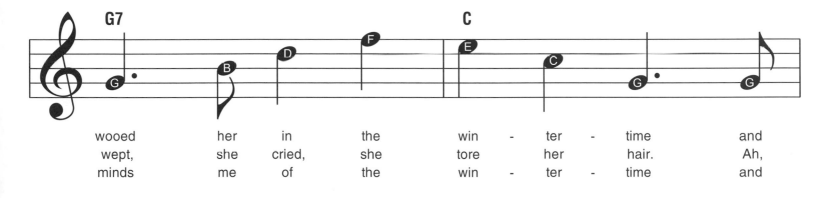

wooed her in the win - ter - time and
wept, she cried, she tore her hair. Ah,
minds me of the win - ter - time and

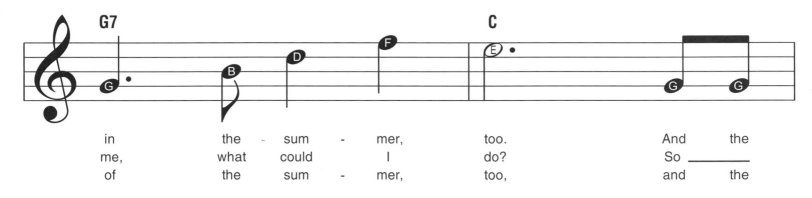

in the sum - mer, too. And the
me, what could I do? So _____
of the sum - mer, too, and the

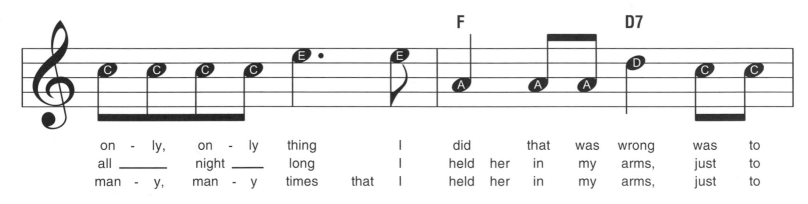

on - ly, on - ly thing I did that was wrong was to
all _____ night _____ long I held her in my arms, just to
man - y, man - y times that I held her in my arms, just to

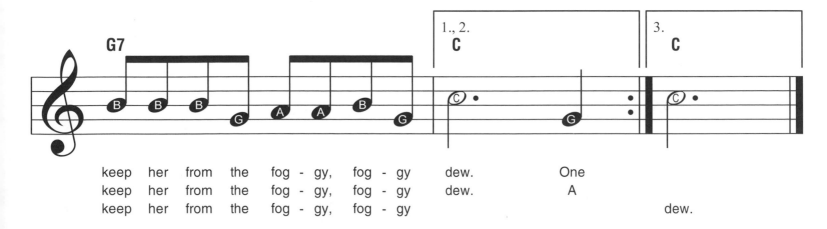

keep her from the fog - gy, fog - gy dew. One
keep her from the fog - gy, fog - gy dew. A
keep her from the fog - gy, fog - gy dew.

For He's a Jolly Good Fellow

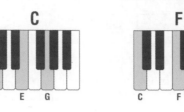
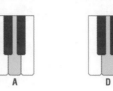
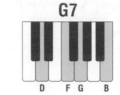

Traditional

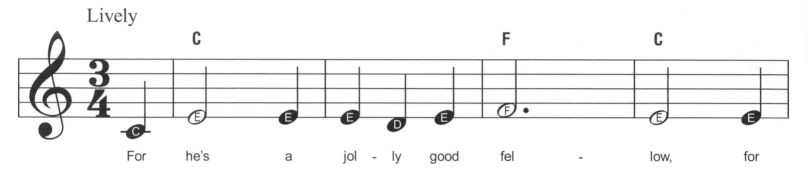

For he's a jol - ly good fel - low, for

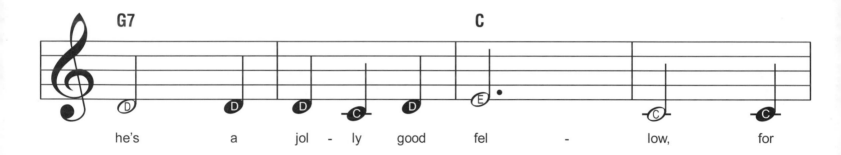

he's a jol - ly good fel - low, for

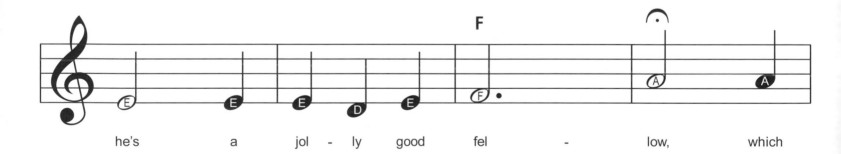

he's a jol - ly good fel - low, which

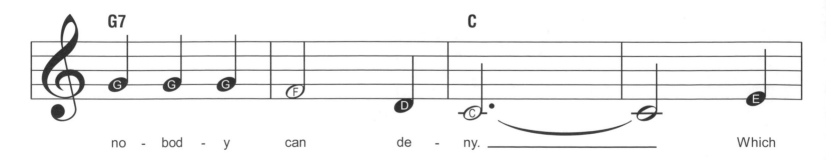

no - bod - y can de - ny. _____ Which

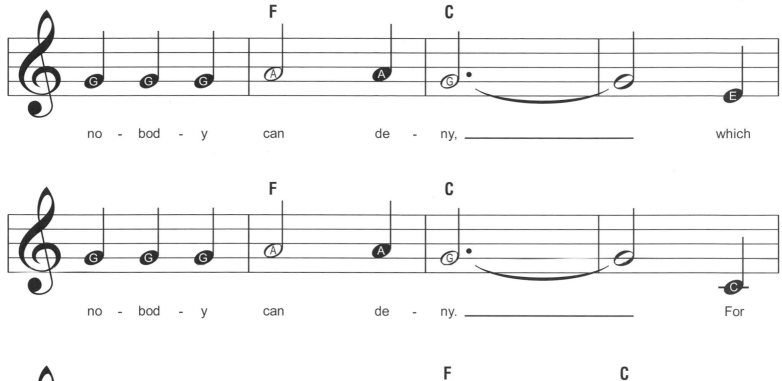

no - bod - y can de - ny, _____ which

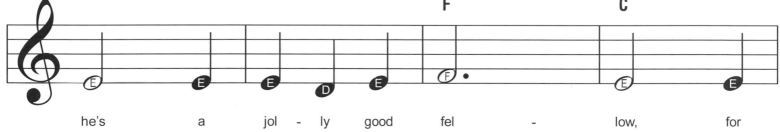

no - bod - y can de - ny. _____ For

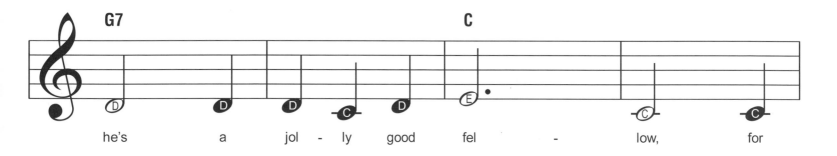

he's a jol - ly good fel - low, for

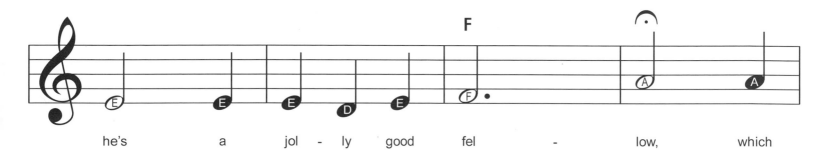

he's a jol - ly good fel - low, for

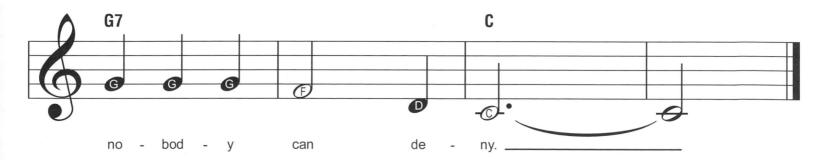

he's a jol - ly good fel - low, which

no - bod - y can de - ny. _____

Frère Jacques
(Are You Sleeping?)

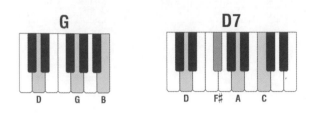

Traditional

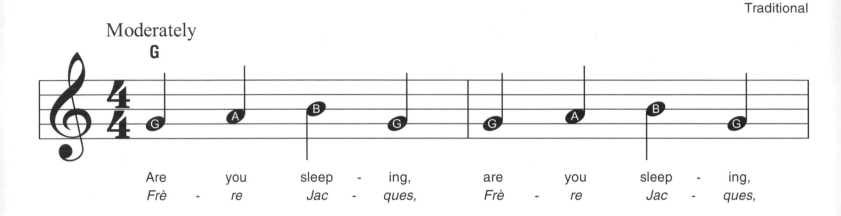

Moderately

Are you sleep - ing, are you sleep - ing,
Frè - re Jac - ques, Frè - re Jac - ques,

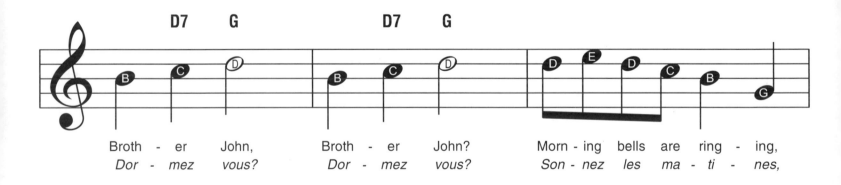

Broth - er John, Broth - er John? Morn - ing bells are ring - ing,
Dor - mez vous? Dor - mez vous? Son - nez les ma - ti - nes,

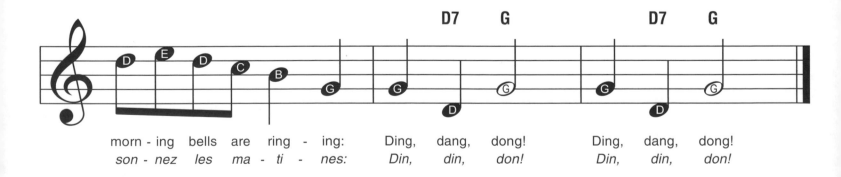

morn - ing bells are ring - ing: Ding, dang, dong! Ding, dang, dong!
son - nez les ma - ti - nes: Din, din, don! Din, din, don!

Girl I Left Behind Me

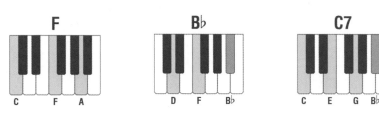

Traditional Irish

The ___ hour was sad I left the maid, a lin-g'ring fare-well ___ tak-ing. Her ___ sighs and tears my steps de-layed, I thought her heart was ___ break-ing. In ___ hur-ried words, her name I blessed. I breathed the vows that bind me, and ___ to my heart in an-guish pressed the girl I left be-hind me.

He's Got the Whole World
in His Hands

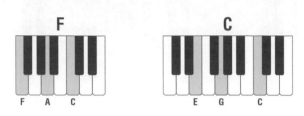

Traditional Spiritual

Additional Lyrics

2. He's got the wind and the rain in His hands. *(3x)*
   He's got the whole world in His hands.

3. He's got the little tiny baby in His hands. *(3x)*
   He's got the whole world in His hands.

4. He's got everybody here in His hands. *(3x)*
   He's got the whole world in His hands.

Hush, Little Baby

Carolina Folk Lullaby

Home on the Range

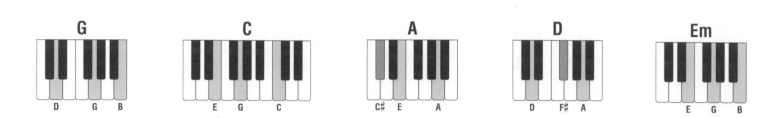

Lyrics by Dr. Brewster Higley
Music by Dan Kelly

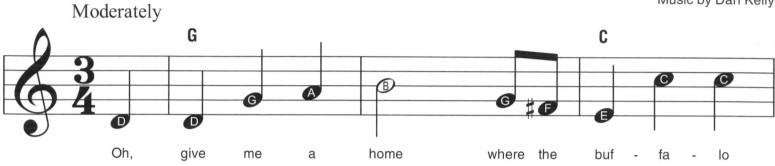

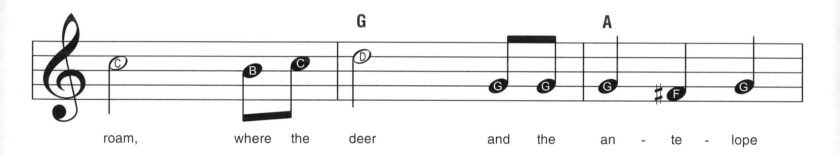

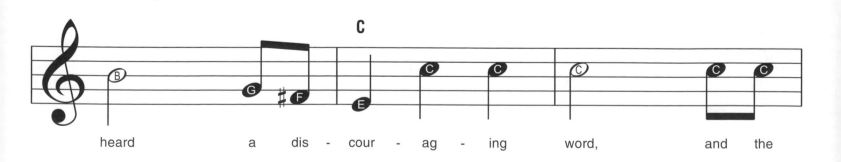

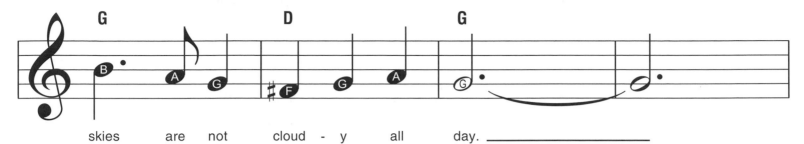

skies are not cloud - y all day. _____

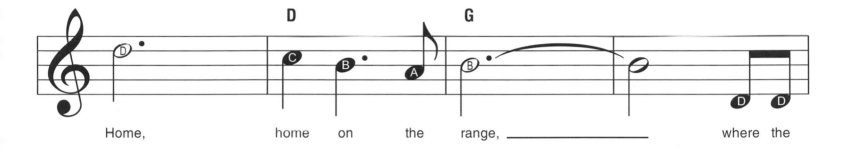

Home, home on the range, _____ where the

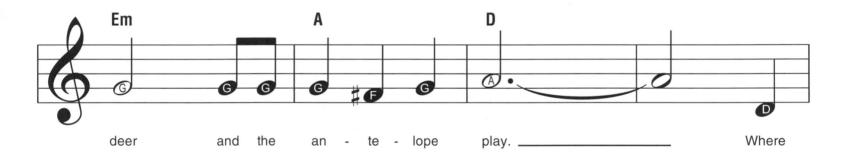

deer and the an - te - lope play. _____ Where

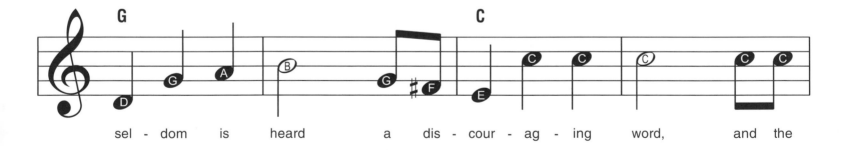

sel - dom is heard a dis - cour - ag - ing word, and the

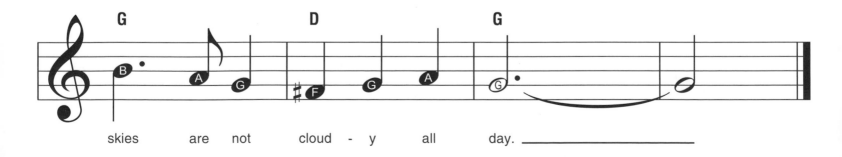

skies are not cloud - y all day. _____

52

Home Sweet Home

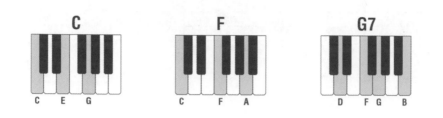

Words by John Howard Payne
Music by Henry R. Bishop

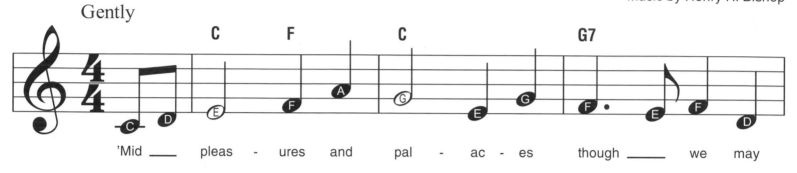

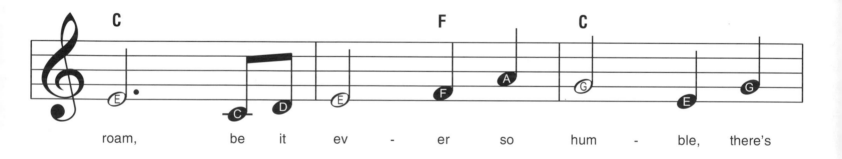

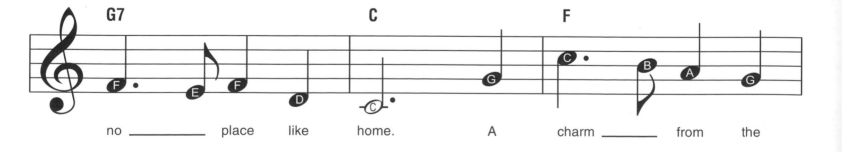

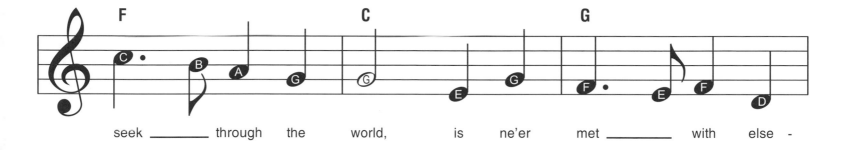

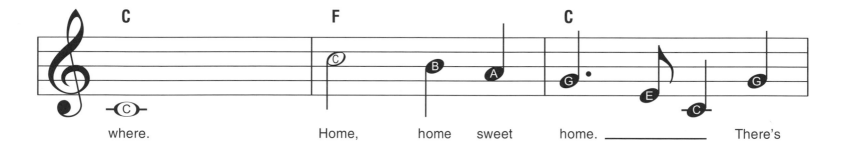

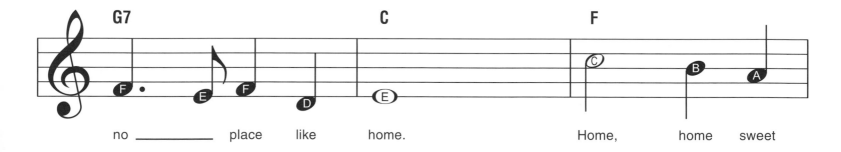

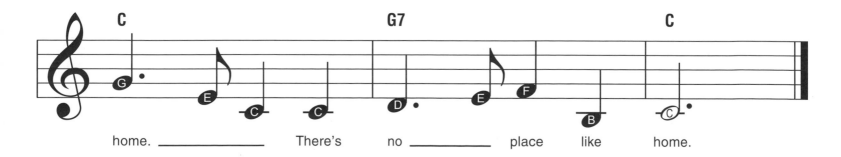

I Gave My Love a Cherry
(The Riddle Song)

G   C   D

D G B   E G C   D F# A

Traditional

Moderately

I gave my love a cher - ry that had no stone. I
How can there be a cher - ry that has no stone? How
A cher - ry when it's bloom - ing, it has no stone. A

gave my love a chick - en that had no bone. I
can there be a chick - en that has no bone? How
chick - en when it's pip - ping, it has no bone. The

told my love a sto - ry that had no end. I
can there be a sto - ry that has no end? How
sto - ry that I love you, it has no end. A

gave my love a ba - by with no cry - in'.
can there be a ba - by with no cry - in'?
ba - by, when it's sleep - ing, has no cry - in'.

Pop Goes the Weasel

Traditional

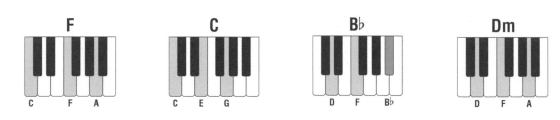

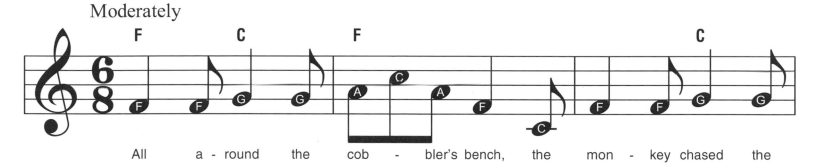

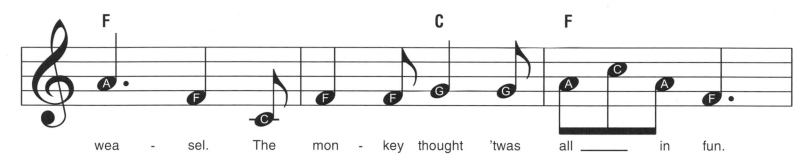

All a-round the cob - bler's bench, the mon - key chased the

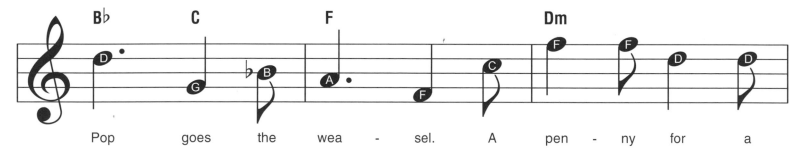

wea - sel. The mon - key thought 'twas all _____ in fun.

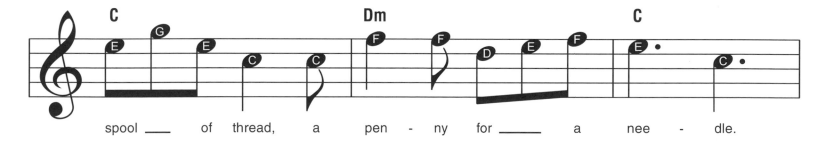

Pop goes the wea - sel. A pen - ny for a

spool ___ of thread, a pen - ny for _____ a nee - dle.

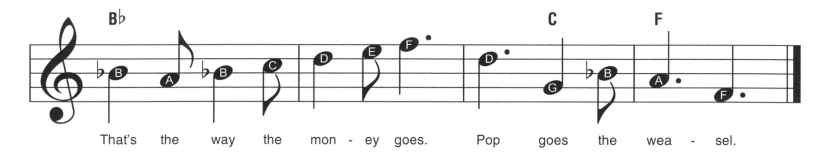

That's the way the mon - ey goes. Pop goes the wea - sel.

Jeanie with the Light Brown Hair

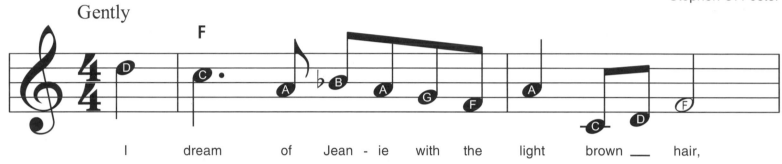

Words and Music by
Stephen C. Foster

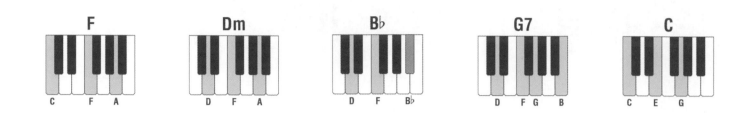

Gently

I dream of Jean - ie with the light brown ___ hair,

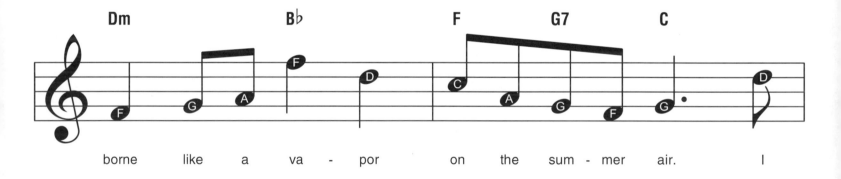

borne like a va - por on the sum - mer air. I

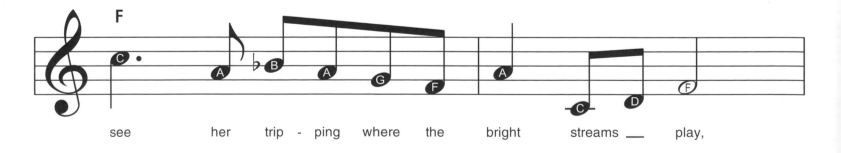

see her trip - ping where the bright streams ___ play,

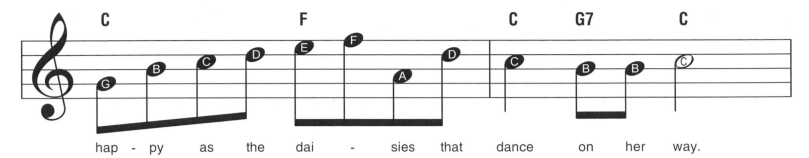

hap - py as the dai - sies that dance on her way.

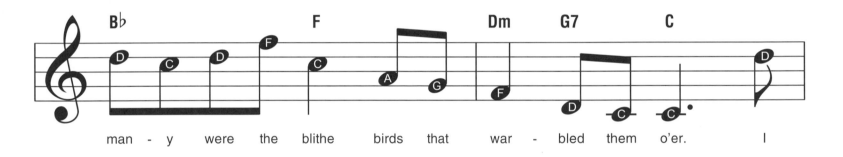

Man - y were the wild notes her mer - ry voice would pour,

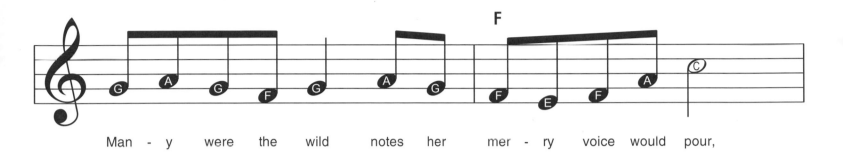

man - y were the blithe birds that war - bled them o'er. I

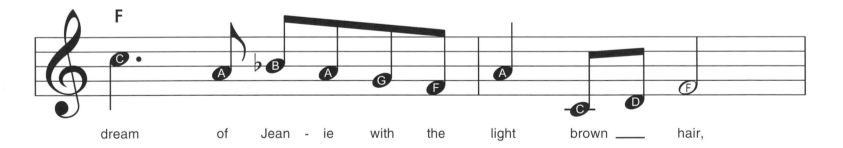

dream of Jean - ie with the light brown ___ hair,

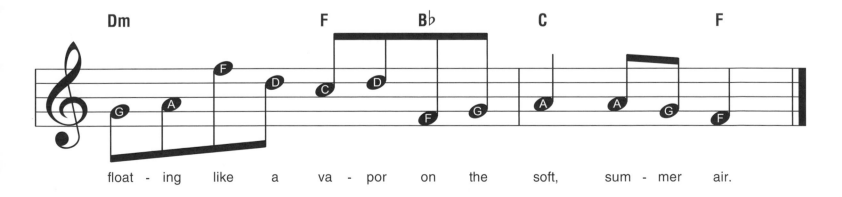

float - ing like a va - por on the soft, sum - mer air.

My Bonnie Lies Over the Ocean

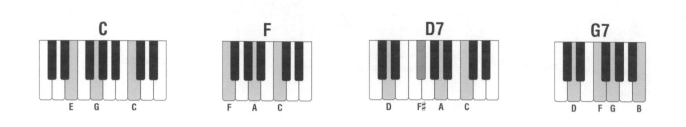

Traditional

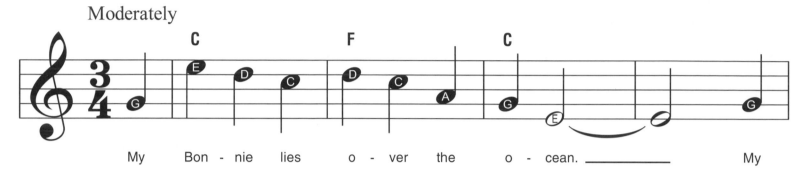

Moderately

My Bon - nie lies o - ver the o - cean. _____ My

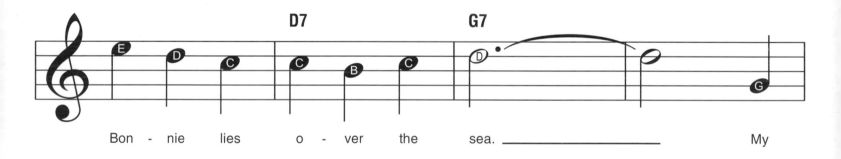

Bon - nie lies o - ver the sea. _____ My

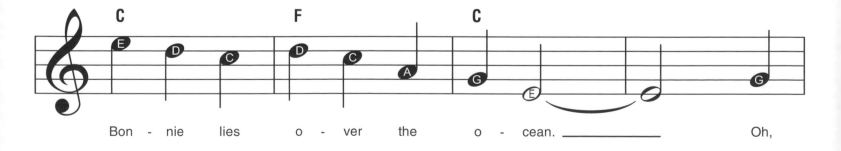

Bon - nie lies o - ver the o - cean. _____ Oh,

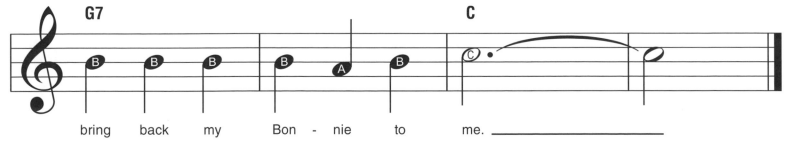

My Wild Irish Rose

By Chauncey Olcott

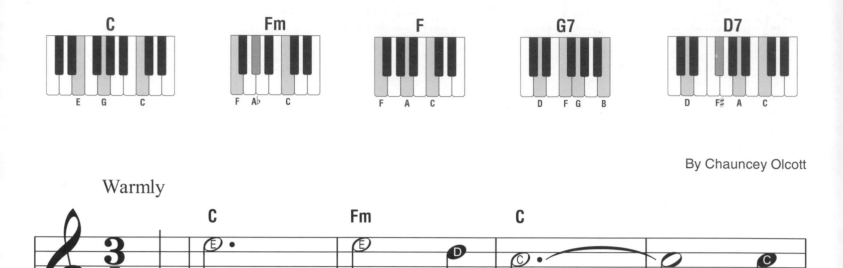

Warmly

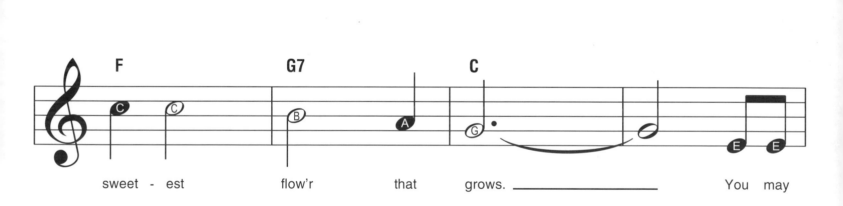

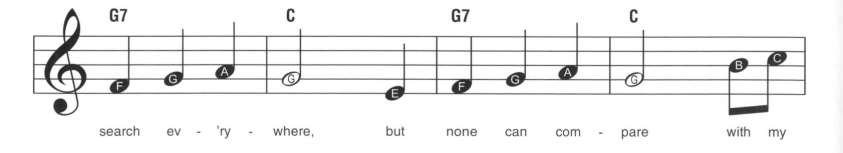

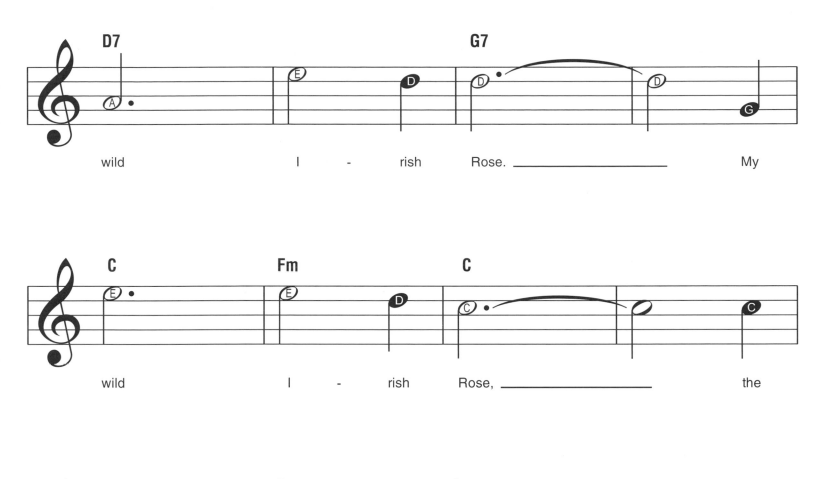

wild   I - rish   Rose. _____   My

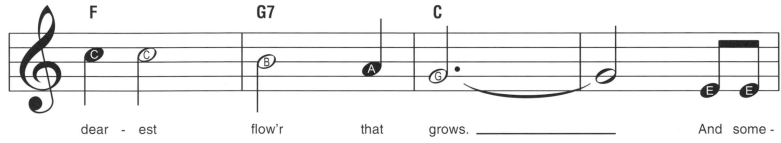

wild   I - rish   Rose, _____   the

dear - est   flow'r   that   grows. _____   And   some -

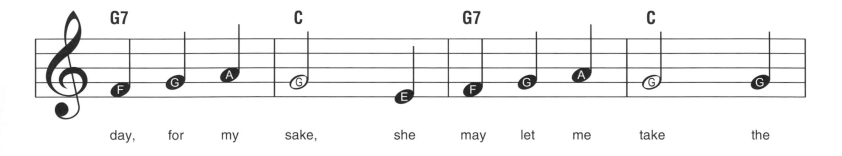

day,   for   my   sake,   she   may   let   me   take   the

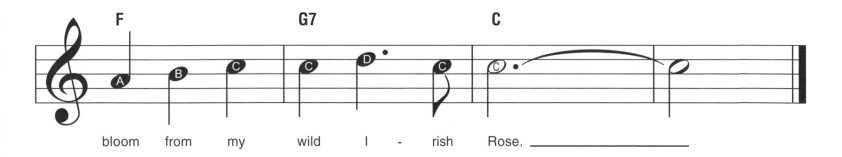

bloom   from   my   wild   I - rish   Rose. _____

Nobody Knows the Trouble I've Seen

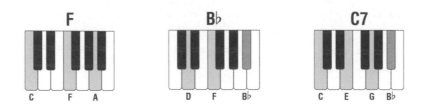

African-American Spiritual

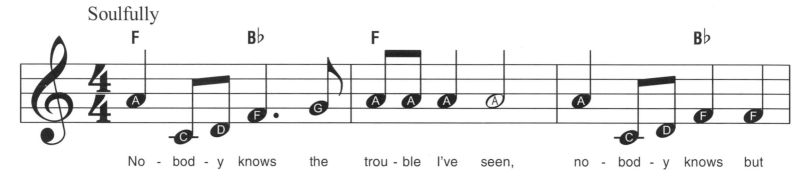

No - bod - y knows the trou - ble I've seen, no - bod - y knows but

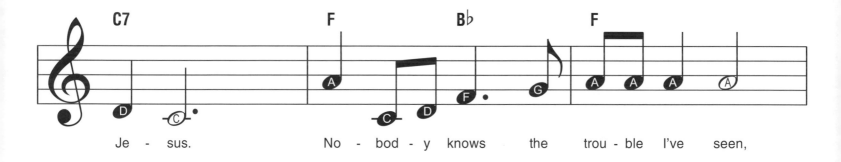

Je - sus. No - bod - y knows the trou - ble I've seen,

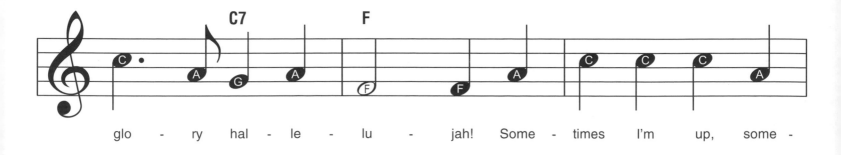

glo - ry hal - le - lu - jah! Some - times I'm up, some -

63

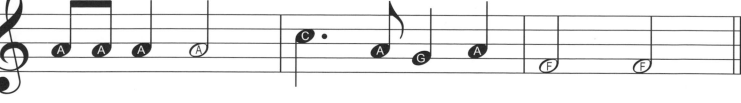

'O Sole Mio

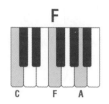
F

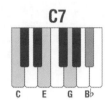
Gm

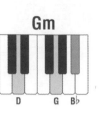
C7

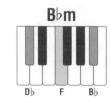
Bbm

Words by Giovanni Capurro
Music by Eduardo di Capua

Moderately

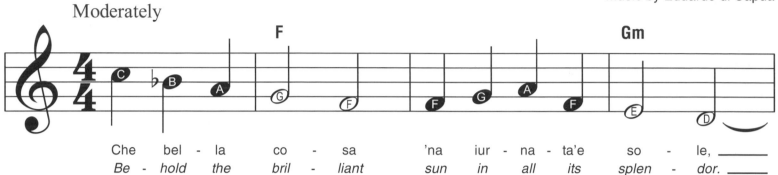

Che bel - la co - sa 'na iur - na - ta'e so - le, _____
Be - hold the bril - liant sun in all its splen - dor. _____

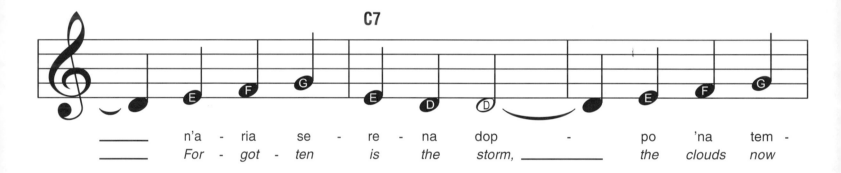

_____ n'a - ria se - re - na dop - po 'na tem -
For - got - ten is the storm, _____ the clouds now

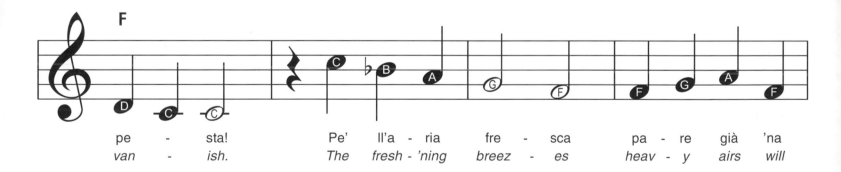

pe - sta! Pe' ll'a - ria fre - sca pa - re già 'na
van - ish. The fresh - 'ning breez - es heav - y airs will

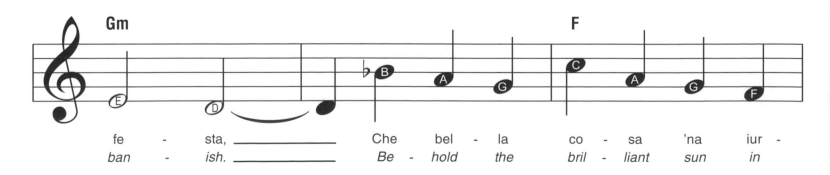

fe - sta, _____ Che bel - la co - sa 'na iur -
ban - ish. _____ Be - hold the bril - liant sun in

na - ta'e so - le.   Ma n'a - tu
all   its   splen - dor.   *A   sun   I*

so - le   cchiù bel - lo, ohi - ne',   'o so - le
know   of   that's bright - er   still.   *This sun, my*

mi - o   sta - 'nfron - te a   te!   'O
dear - est,   *is   naught but! thee.*   *Thy*

so -   le 'o so - le mi - o   sta - nfron - te a
face   *so fair to   see,   that*   *shall now my*

te,   sta - 'nfron - te a te! _____
sun   *for - ev - er   be!* _____

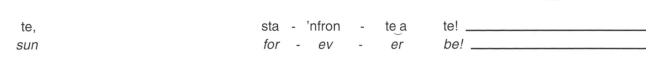

The Red River Valley

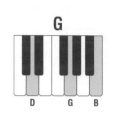
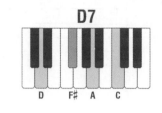
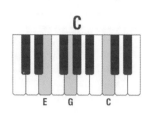

Traditional American Cowboy Song

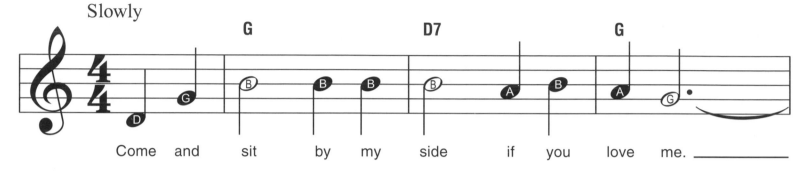

Come and sit by my side if you love me. _____

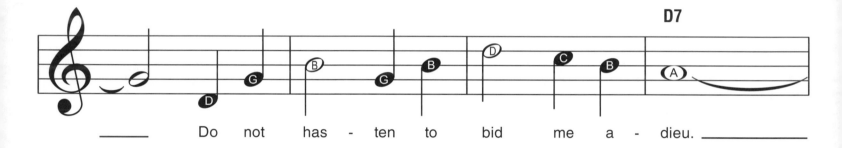

_____ Do not has - ten to bid me a - dieu. _____

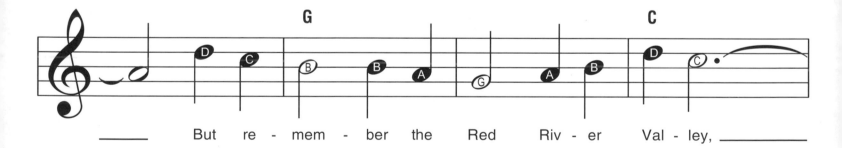

_____ But re - mem - ber the Red Riv - er Val - ley, _____

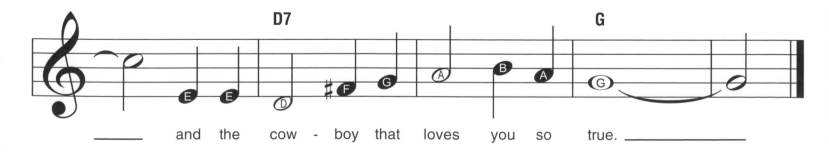

_____ and the cow - boy that loves you so true. _____

Rock-a-Bye, Baby

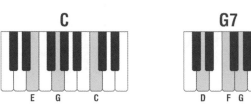

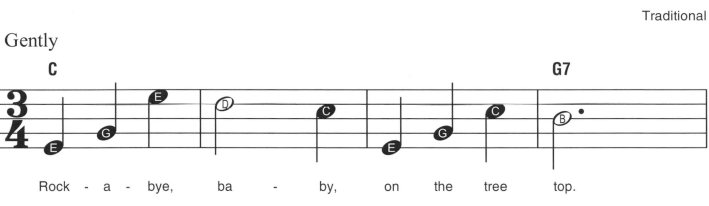

Traditional

Gently

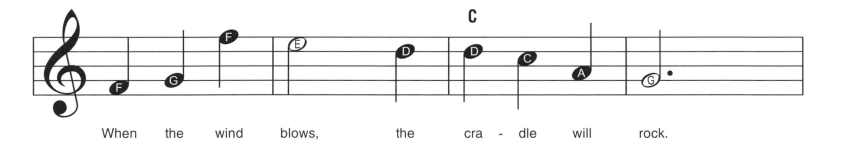

Rock - a - bye, ba - by, on the tree top.

When the wind blows, the cra - dle will rock.

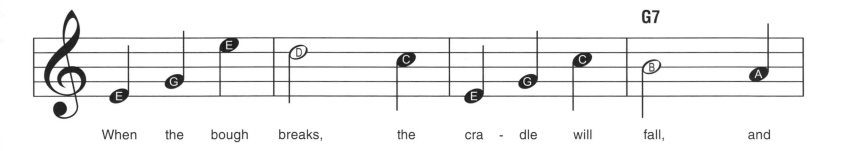

When the bough breaks, the cra - dle will fall, and

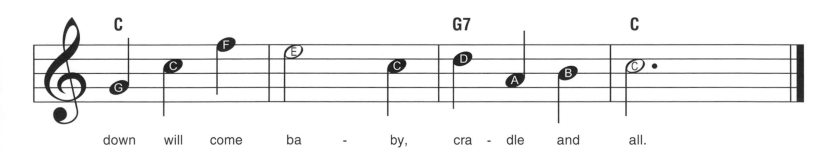

down will come ba - by, cra - dle and all.

Sailing, Sailing

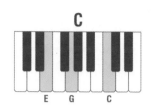
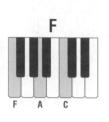
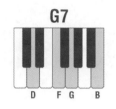
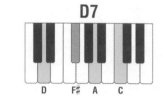

Words and Music by
Godfrey Marks

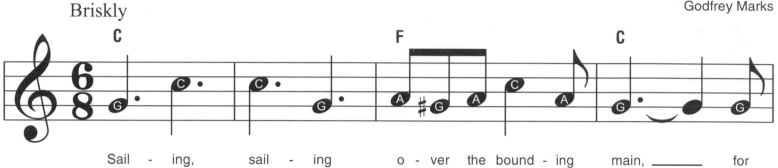

Sail - ing, sail - ing o - ver the bound - ing main, _____ for

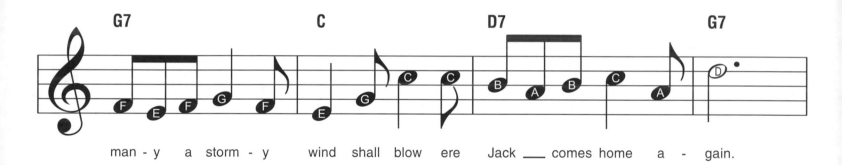

man - y a storm - y wind shall blow ere Jack ___ comes home a - gain.

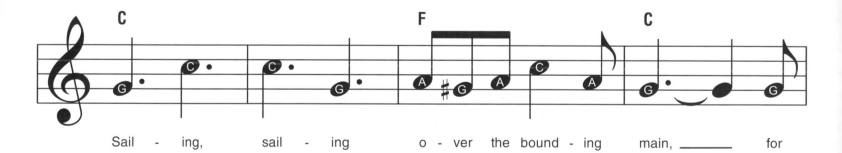

Sail - ing, sail - ing o - ver the bound - ing main, _____ for

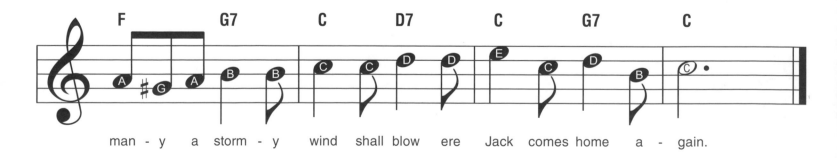

man - y a storm - y wind shall blow ere Jack comes home a - gain.

Sakura
(Cherry Blossoms)

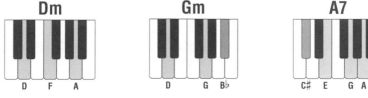

Traditional Japanese Folksong

Santa Lucia

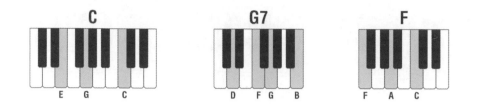

By Teodoro Cottrau

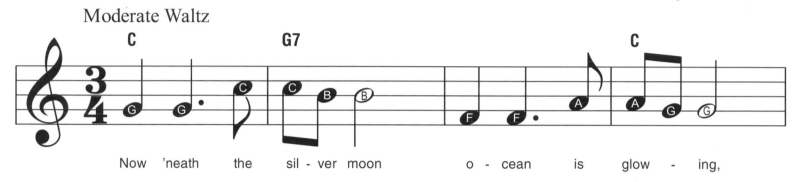

Moderate Waltz

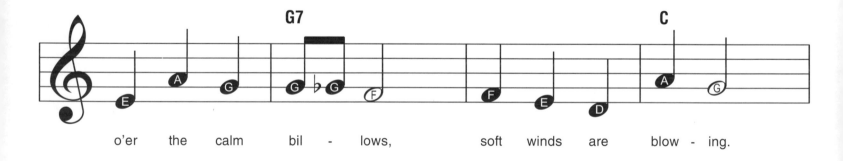

Now 'neath the sil - ver moon o - cean is glow - ing,

o'er the calm bil - lows, soft winds are blow - ing.

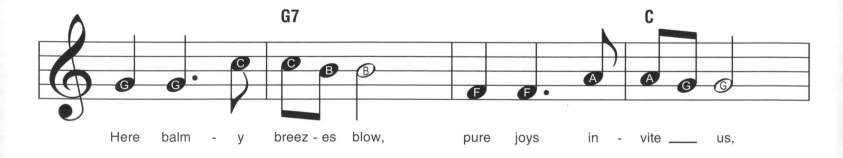

Here balm - y breez - es blow, pure joys in - vite ___ us,

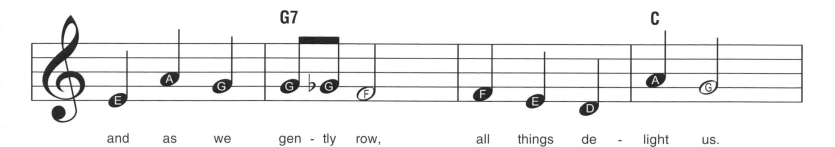

and as we gen - tly row, all things de - light us.

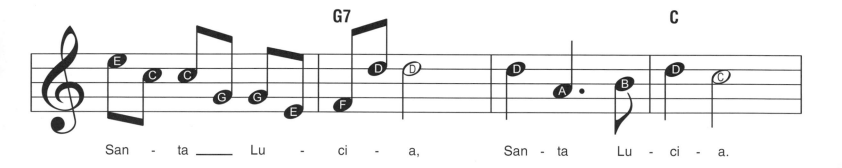

Hark! how the sail - ors cry, joy - ous - ly ech - oes nigh,

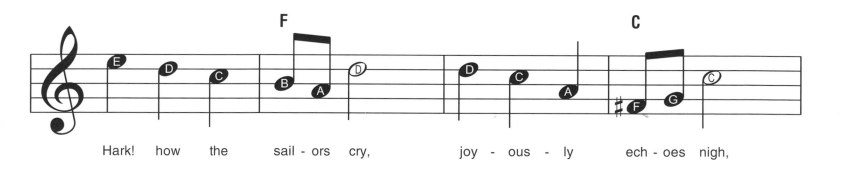

San - ta ____ Lu - ci - a, San - ta Lu - ci - a.

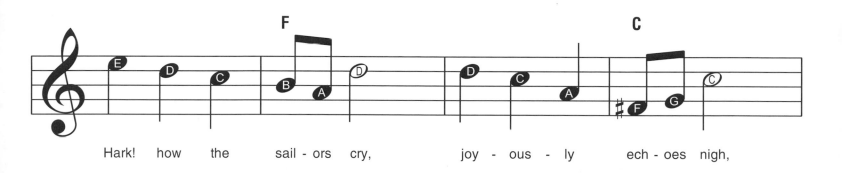

Hark! how the sail - ors cry, joy - ous - ly ech - oes nigh,

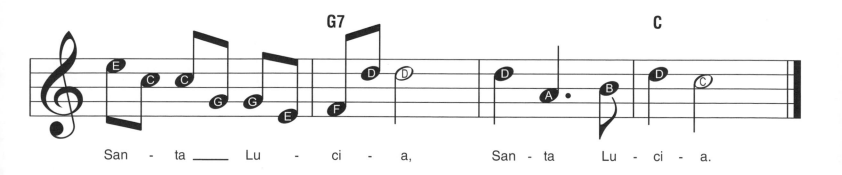

San - ta ____ Lu - ci - a, San - ta Lu - ci - a.

Scarborough Fair

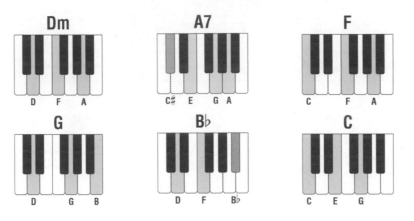

Traditional English

Gently

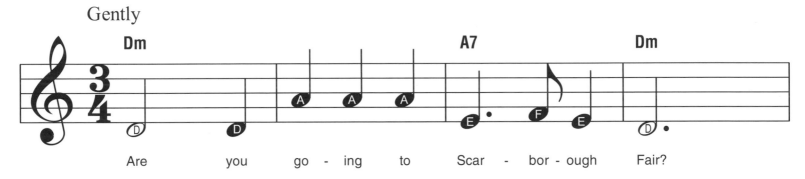

Are you go - ing to Scar - bor - ough Fair?

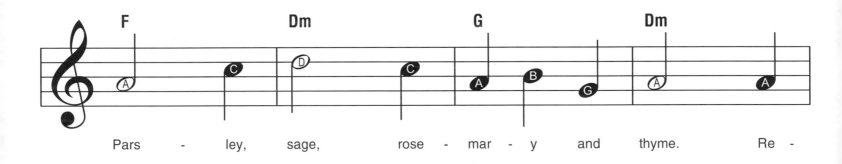

Pars - ley, sage, rose - mar - y and thyme. Re -

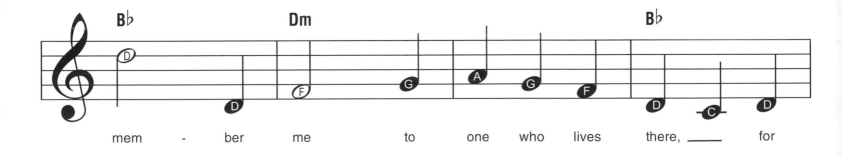

mem - ber me to one who lives there, _____ for

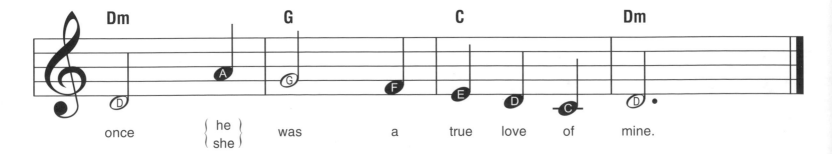

once { he } { she } was a true love of mine.

She'll Be Comin'
'Round the Mountain

Traditional

Shenandoah

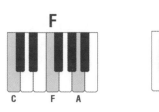
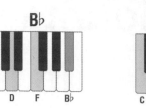
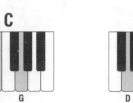
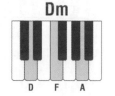

American Folksong

Gentle half-time feel

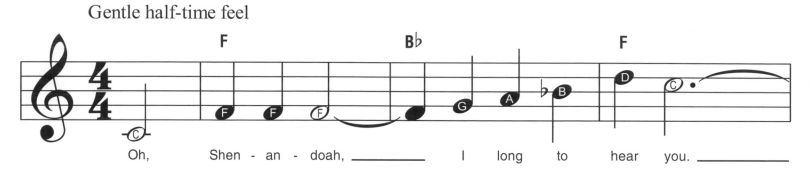

Oh, Shen - an - doah, _____ I long to hear you. _____

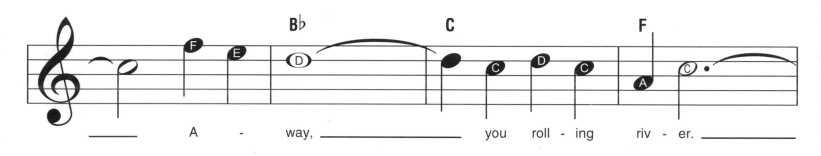

_____ A - way, _____ you roll - ing riv - er. _____

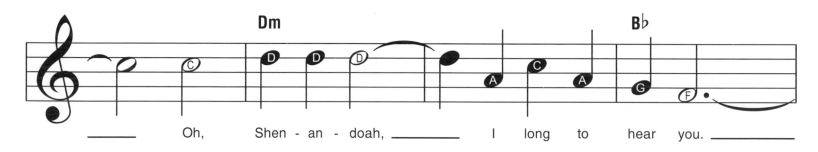

_____ Oh, Shen - an - doah, _____ I long to hear you. _____

_____ A - way, _____ we're bound a - way, _____

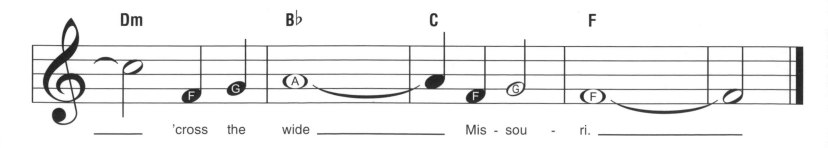

_____ 'cross the wide _____ Mis - sou - ri. _____

Sing a Song of Sixpence

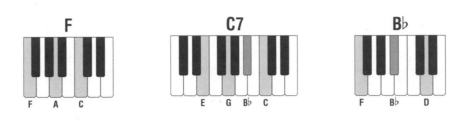

Traditional

Sing a song of six - pence, a pock - et full of rye.

Four and twen - ty black - birds baked in a pie.

When the pie was o - pened, the birds be - gan to sing.

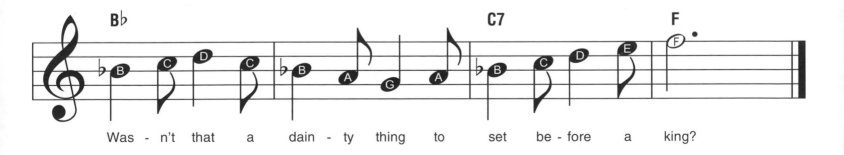

Was - n't that a dain - ty thing to set be - fore a king?

Simple Gifts

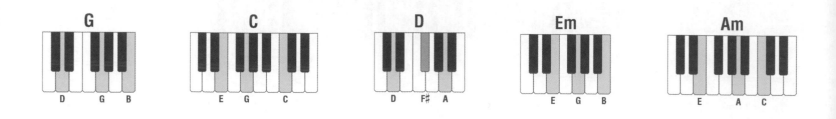

Traditional Shaker Hymn

Warmly

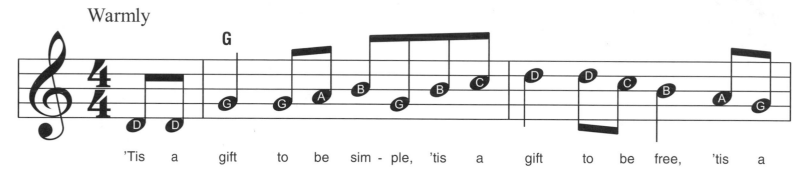

'Tis a gift to be sim - ple, 'tis a gift to be free, 'tis a

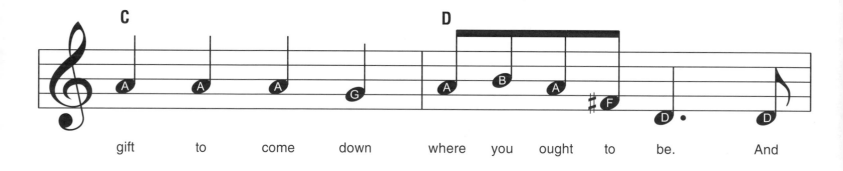

gift to come down where you ought to be. And

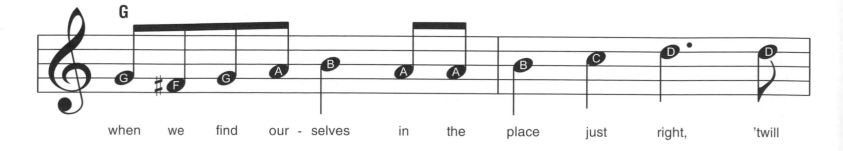

when we find our - selves in the place just right, 'twill

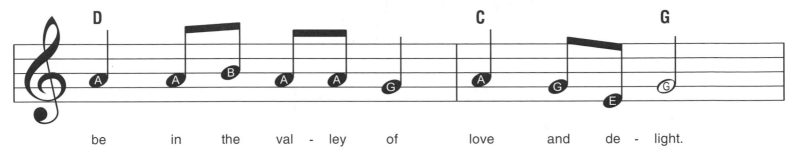

be in the val - ley of love and de - light.

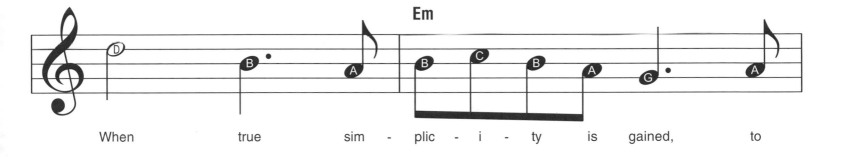

When true sim - plic - i - ty is gained, to

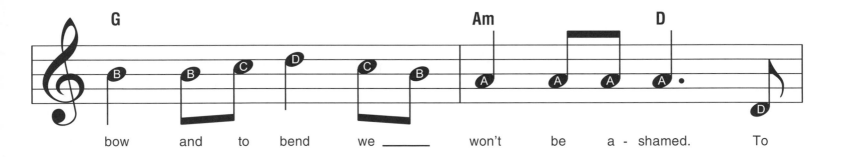

bow and to bend we ____ won't be a - shamed. To

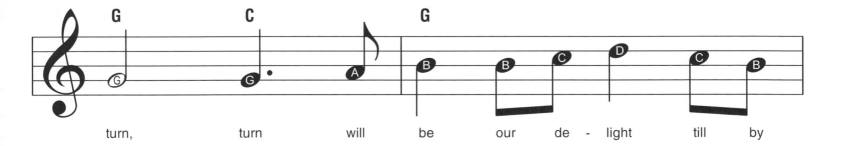

turn, turn will be our de - light till by

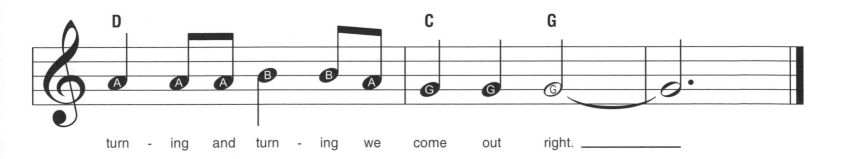

turn - ing and turn - ing we come out right. ____

Skip to My Lou

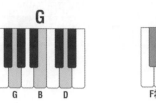

Traditional

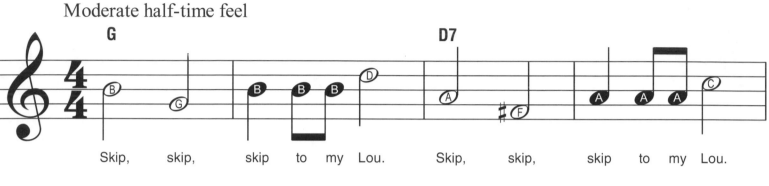

Moderate half-time feel

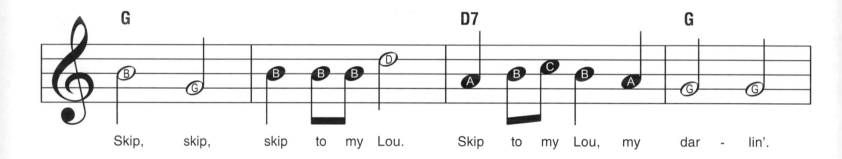

Skip, skip, skip to my Lou. Skip, skip, skip to my Lou.

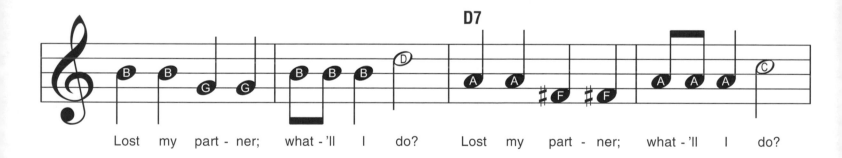

Skip, skip, skip to my Lou. Skip to my Lou, my dar - lin'.

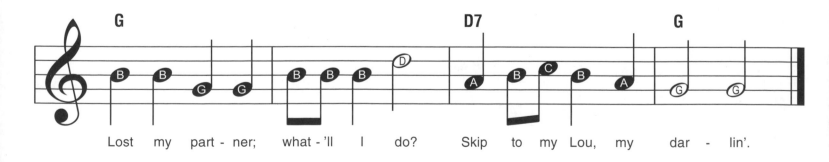

Lost my part - ner; what - 'll I do? Lost my part - ner; what - 'll I do?

Lost my part - ner; what - 'll I do? Skip to my Lou, my dar - lin'.

The Streets of Laredo

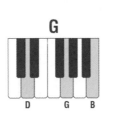
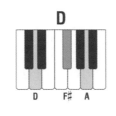
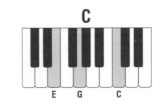

American Cowboy Song

Swing Low, Sweet Chariot

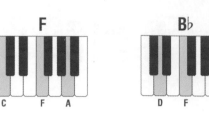
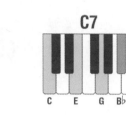
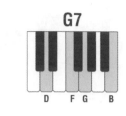

Traditional Spiritual

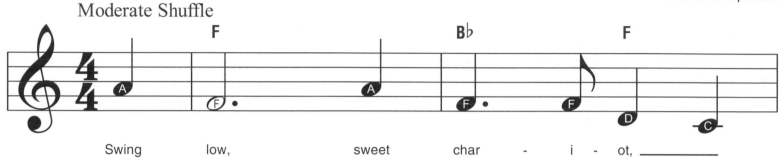

Swing low, sweet char - i - ot, _____

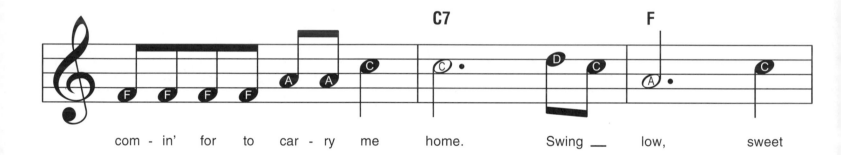

com - in' for to car - ry me home. Swing __ low, sweet

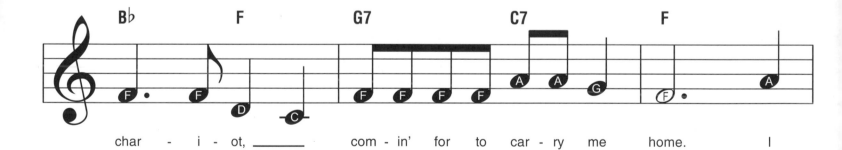

char - i - ot, _____ com - in' for to car - ry me home. I

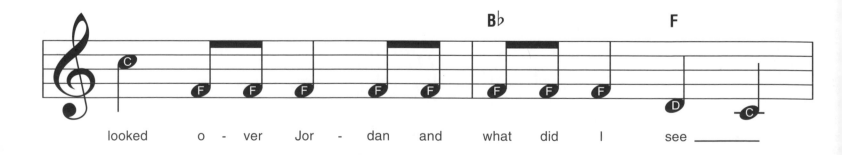

looked o - ver Jor - dan and what did I see _____

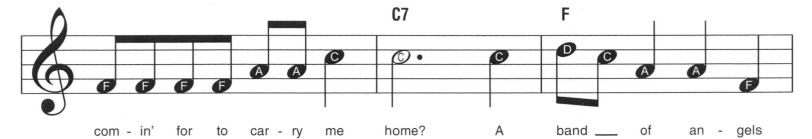

com - in' for to car - ry me home? A band ___ of an - gels

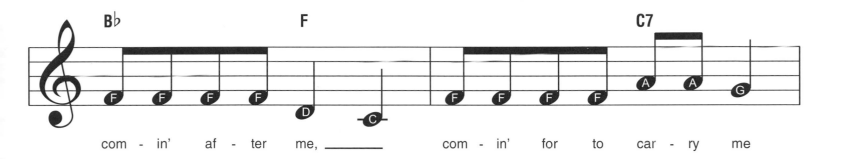

com - in' af - ter me, _____ com - in' for to car - ry me

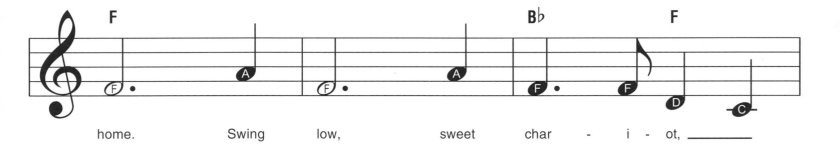

home. Swing low, sweet char - i - ot, _____

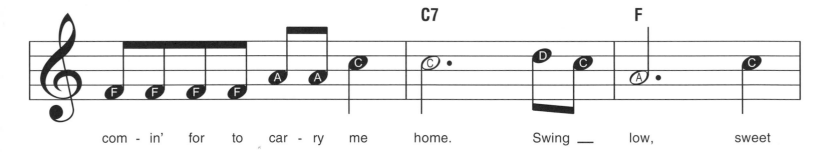

com - in' for to car - ry me home. Swing ___ low, sweet

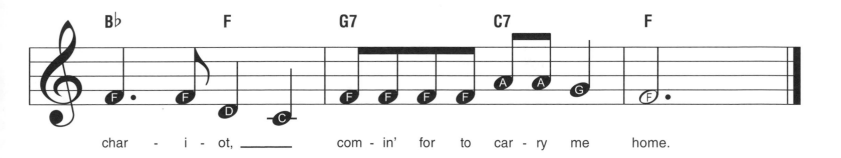

char - i - ot, _____ com - in' for to car - ry me home.

Take Me Out to the Ball Game

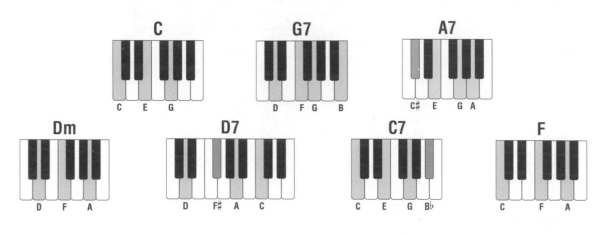

Words by Jack Norworth
Music by Albert von Tilzer

Brightly

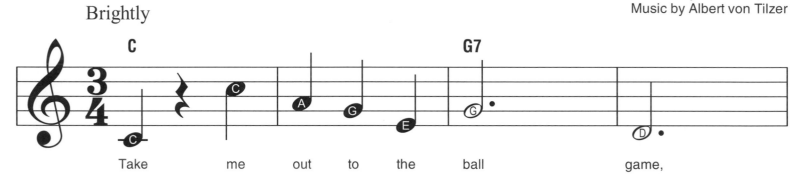

Take me out to the ball game,

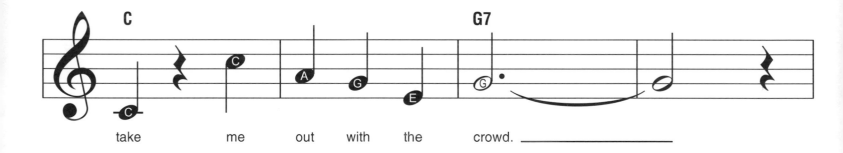

take me out with the crowd. _____

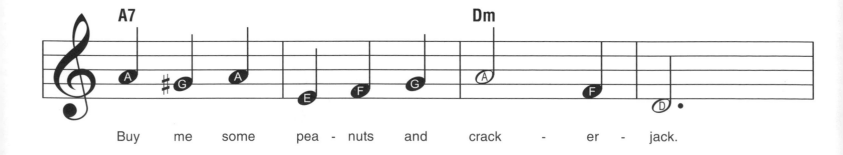

Buy me some pea - nuts and crack - er - jack.

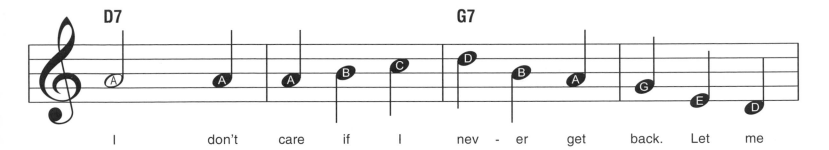

I don't care if I nev-er get back. Let me

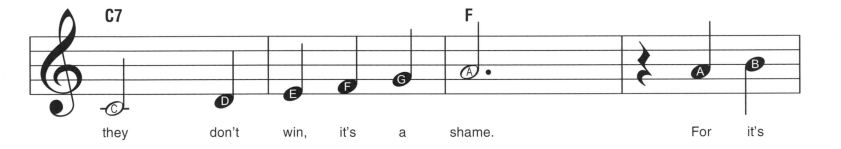

root, root, root for the home team. If

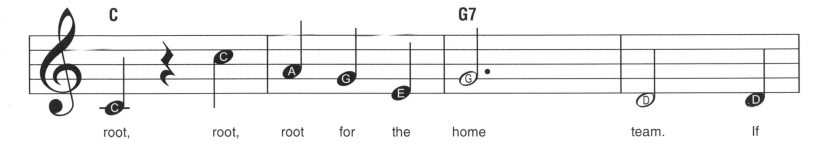

they don't win, it's a shame. For it's

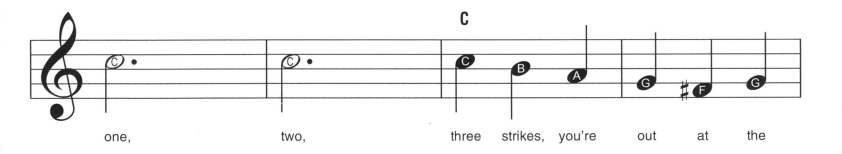

one, two, three strikes, you're out at the

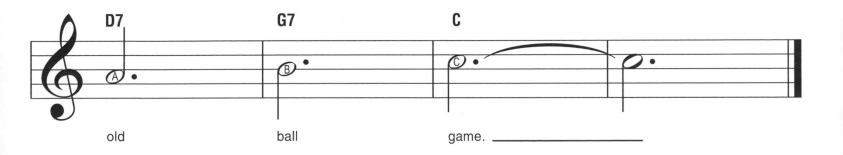

old ball game. _____

Turkey in the Straw

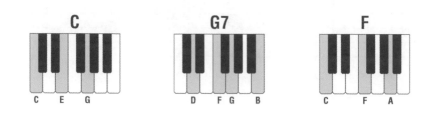

American Folksong

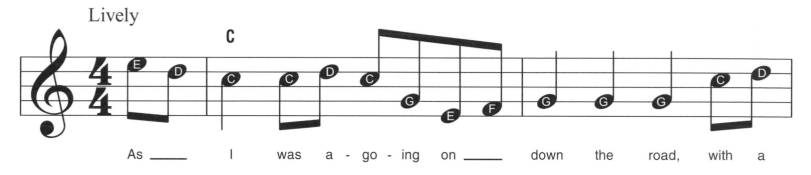

As ____ I was a - go - ing on ____ down the road, with a

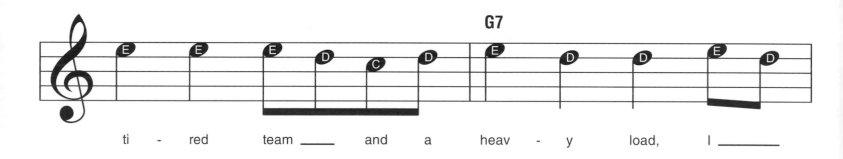

ti - red team ____ and a heav - y load, I ____

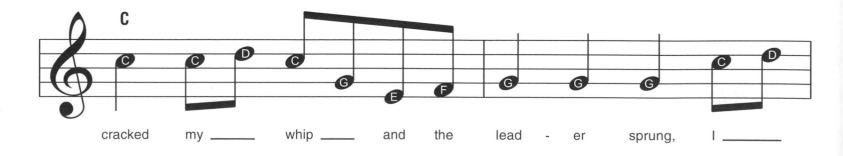

cracked my ____ whip ____ and the lead - er sprung, I ____

says day - day _____ to the wag - on tongue.

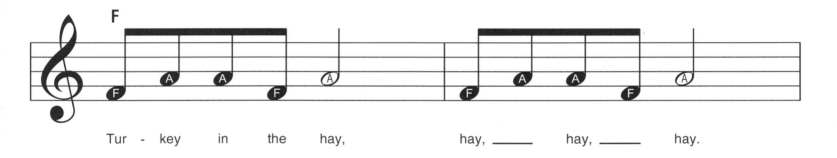

Tur - key in the straw, haw, _____ haw, _____ haw.

Tur - key in the hay, hay, _____ hay, _____ hay.

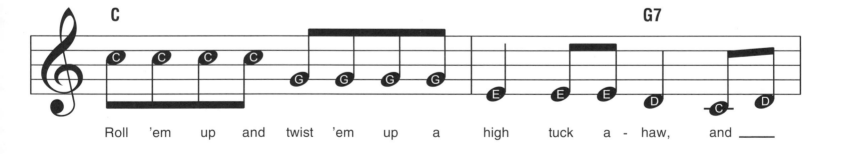

Roll 'em up and twist 'em up a high tuck a - haw, and _____

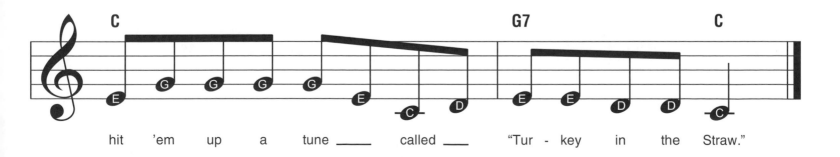

hit 'em up a tune _____ called _____ "Tur - key in the Straw."

The Wabash Cannon Ball

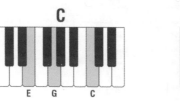
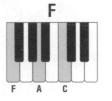
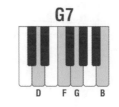

Hobo Song

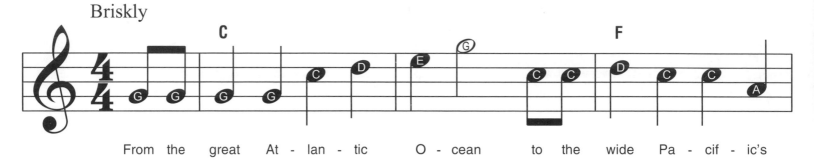

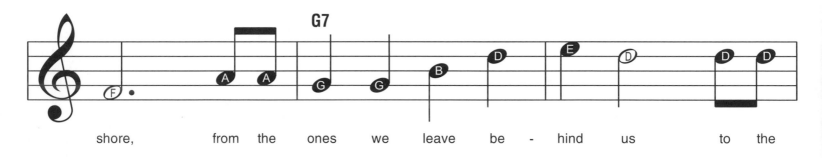

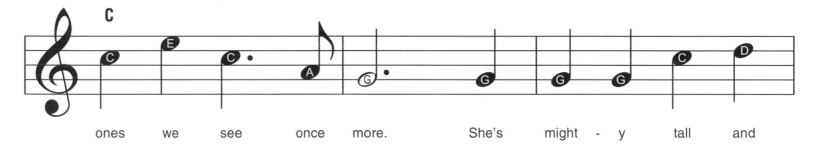

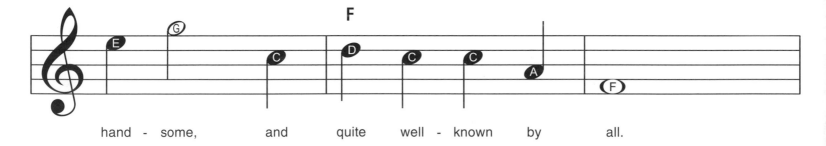

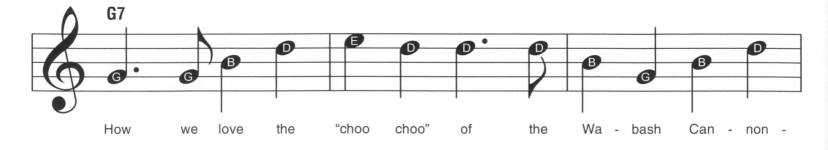

ball.   Hear the bell and whis - tle

call - ing,   hear the wheels that go "clack clack."   Hear the

roar - ing of the en - gine as she rolls a - long the

track.   The mag - ic of the rail - road wins

hearts of one and all,   as we reach our des - ti -

na - tion on   the Wa - bash Can - non - ball.

Water Is Wide

Traditional

Wellerman

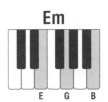
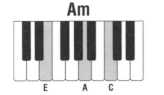
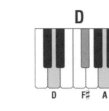
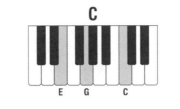
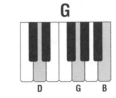

New Zealand Folksong

Lively Sea Shanty

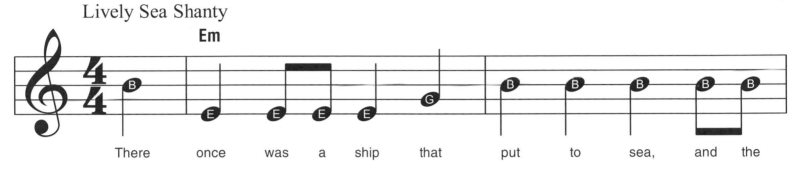

There once was a ship that put to sea, and the

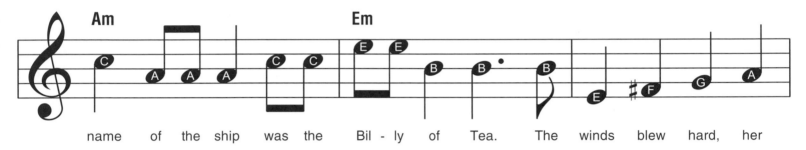

name of the ship was the Bil-ly of Tea. The winds blew hard, her

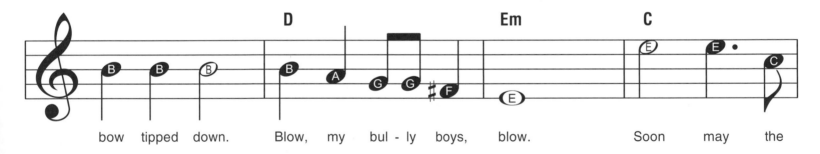

bow tipped down. Blow, my bul-ly boys, blow. Soon may the

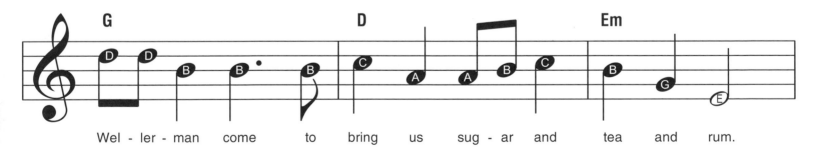

Wel-ler-man come to bring us sug-ar and tea and rum.

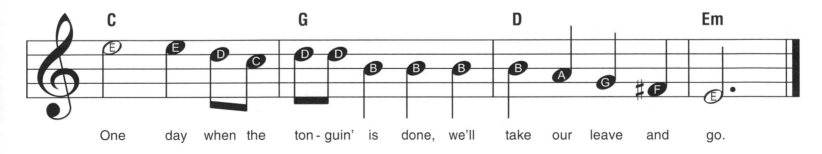

One day when the ton-guin' is done, we'll take our leave and go.

Wayfaring Stranger

Southern American Folk Hymn

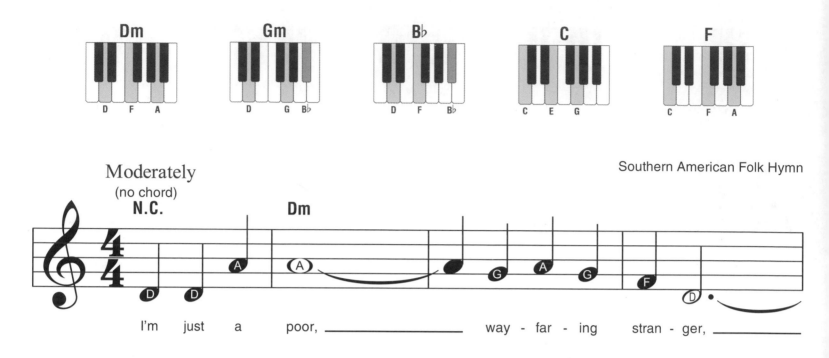

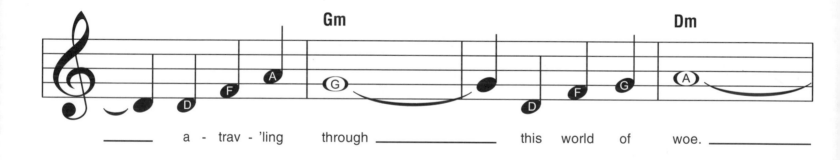

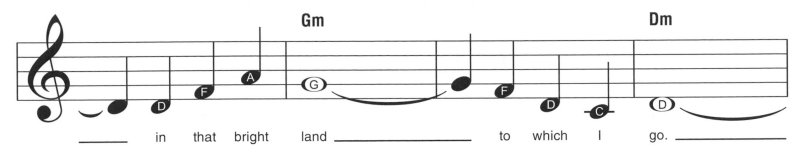

in that bright land _____ to which I go. _____

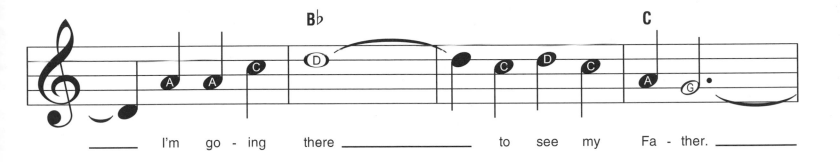

_____ I'm go - ing there _____ to see my Fa - ther. _____

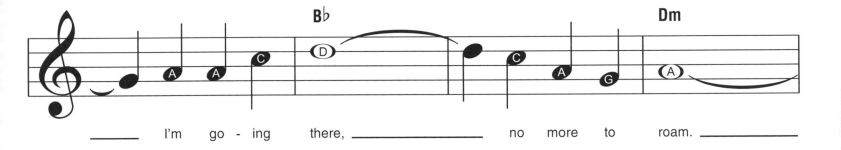

_____ I'm go - ing there, _____ no more to roam. _____

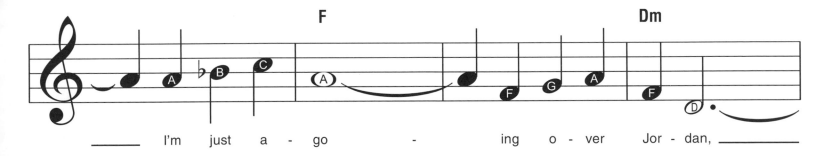

_____ I'm just a - go - ing o - ver Jor - dan, _____

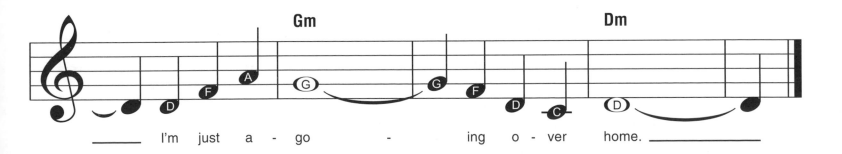

_____ I'm just a - go - ing o - ver home. _____

When Johnny Comes Marching Home

Words and Music by
Patrick Sarsfield Gilmore

When the Saints Go Marching In

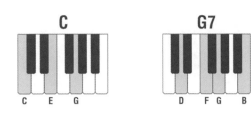
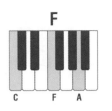

Words by Katherine E. Purvis
Music by James M. Black

The Yellow Rose of Texas

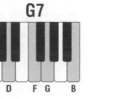
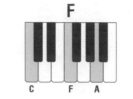

Words and Music by
J.K., 1858

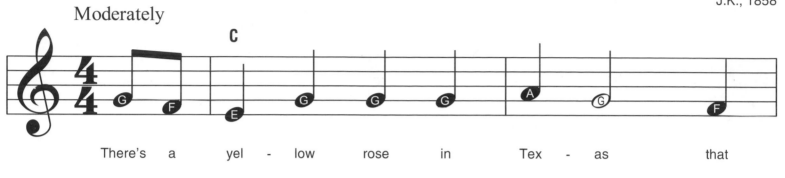

There's a yel - low rose in Tex - as that

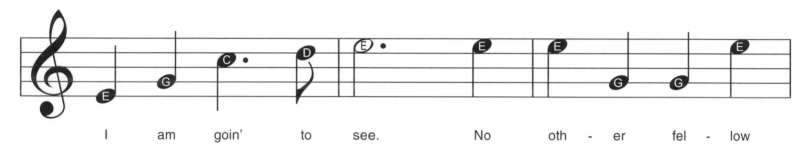

I am goin' to see. No oth - er fel - low

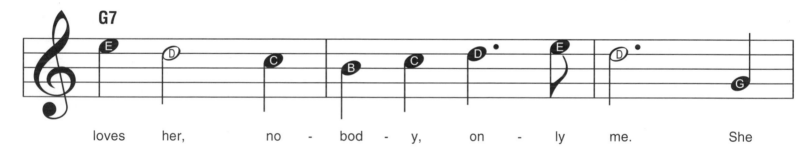

loves her, no - bod - y, on - ly me. She

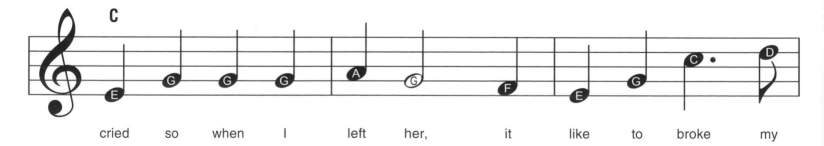

cried so when I left her, it like to broke my

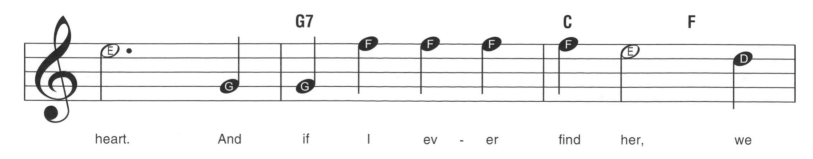

heart. And if I ev - er find her, we

It's super easy! This series features accessible arrangements for piano, with simple right-hand melody, letter names inside each note, and basic left-hand chord diagrams. Perfect for players of all ages!

THE BEATLES
00198161 60 songs $15.99

BEETHOVEN
00345533 21 selections $9.99

BEST SONGS EVER
00329877 60 songs $15.99

BROADWAY
00193871 60 songs $15.99

JOHNNY CASH
00287524 20 songs $9.99

CHRISTMAS CAROLS
00277955 60 songs $15.99

CHRISTMAS SONGS
00236850 60 songs $15.99

CHRISTMAS SONGS WITH 3 CHORDS
00367423 30 songs $10.99

CLASSIC ROCK
00287526 60 songs $15.99

CLASSICAL
00194693 60 selections...............$15.99

COUNTRY
00285257 60 songs $14.99

DISNEY
00199558 60 songs $15.99

BOB DYLAN
00364487 22 songs $12.99

BILLIE EILISH
00346515 22 songs $10.99

FOUR CHORD SONGS
00249533 60 songs $15.99

FROZEN COLLECTION
00334069 14 songs $10.99

GEORGE GERSHWIN
00345536 22 songs $9.99

GOSPEL
00285256 60 songs $15.99

HIT SONGS
00194367 60 songs $15.99

HYMNS
00194659 60 songs $15.99

JAZZ STANDARDS
00233687 60 songs $14.99

BILLY JOEL
00329996 22 songs $10.99

ELTON JOHN
00298762 22 songs $10.99

KIDS' SONGS
00198009 60 songs $14.99

LEAN ON ME
00350593 22 songs $9.99

THE LION KING
00303511 9 songs $9.99

ANDREW LLOYD WEBBER
00249580 48 songs $19.99

MOVIE SONGS
00233670 60 songs $15.99

PEACEFUL MELODIES
00367880 60 songs $16.99

POP SONGS FOR KIDS
00346809 60 songs $16.99

POP STANDARDS
00233770 60 songs $15.99

QUEEN
00294889 20 songs $10.99

ED SHEERAN
00287525 20 songs $9.99

SIMPLE SONGS
00329906 60 songs $15.99

STAR WARS (EPISODES I-IX)
00345560 17 songs $10.99

TAYLOR SWIFT
00323195 22 songs $10.99

THREE CHORD SONGS
00249664 60 songs $15.99

TOP HITS
00300405 22 songs $10.99

WORSHIP
00294871 60 songs $15.99

Disney characters and artwork TM & © 2021 Disney

www.halleonard.com

Prices, contents and availability subject to change without notice.